The Primal Wound

Understanding the Adopted Child

Nancy Newton Verrier

GATEWAY PRESS, INC.
Baltimore, MD

First printing, 1993, Baltimore
Second printing, 1994, Baltimore
Third printing, 1996, Baltimore
Fourth printing, 1997, Baltimore
Fifth printing, 1999, Baltimore
Sixth printing, 2000, Baltimore
Seventh printing, 2002, Baltimore
Eighth printing, 2004, Baltimore

Please direct all correspondence
Nancy Newton Verrier
PO Box 208
Lafayette, CA 94549
www.nancyverrier.com
Library of Congress Catalog Card Number 92-70164
ISBN 0-9636480-0-4

Published for the author by
Gateway Press, Inc.
1001 N. Calvert Street
Baltimore, Maryland 21202

To my daughter
who came into our lives
on a path of sacrifice and pain
yet whose love and courage
have brought us understanding and joy.

CONTENTS

Part IV: Conclusions / 199

ACKNOWLEDGMENTS

This work is a labor of love and dedication on the parts of many people, one which involved pain as well as accomplishment. I want, first of all, to thank all the participants of my original study for delving into parts of their souls which had hitherto been off limits. Their willingness to look at painful aspects of their lives in an honest manner is what made this book possible. My thanks, also, to the many, many adoptees, birthmothers, and adoptive parents who came forward after hearing of my work and added their experiences to those of the original participants. Their response has been overwhelming and their courage exceptional.

I also want to thank those members of the helping professions who gave of their valuable time and knowledge so that I might draw upon a cross-section of experiences having to do with relinquishment and adoption and with bonding and perinatal phenomena. These include Florence Grossenbacher, Jungian analyst, whose work with adoptees in both agency and private settings gave me many insights into problems relating to foster care and adoption; Jean Benward, L.C.S.W., adoptee and psychotherapist, who helped me clarify what it was I wanted to ask adoptees; Dr. David Cheek, M.D., who volunteered to take an adoptee back to the birth and adoption experiences via hypnotic regression; Dr. Thomas Verny, M.D., who took the time to correspond with me about adoption and perinatal experiences; Patricia Ladouceur, Ph.D., adoptee and friend, whose emotional support during this project has been invaluable; and to a trio of friends in adoption B. J. Lifton, Ph.D., Annette Baran, L.C.S.W., and Reuben Pannor, L.C.S.W. with whom I have had great conversations and from whom I have had oodles of encouragement.

I could not have finished this project without the help of several people: my editors Leslie Lauren and Laura Keilin, whose suggestions have made a somewhat clinical subject much more readable for the audience I had in mind; my typist Glenna Goulet, who worked through the holidays to meet my publishing deadline; and my publisher Ann Hughes, whose enthusiasm and dedication to this subject have been very much appreciated. It is interesting that without meaning to I have represented in the above people an adoptee (Leslie), an adoptive mother (Laura), a birthmother (Ann), and the sibling of an adoptee (Glenna). A special thanks to adoptee Jane Schweitzer for the courage it took to bare her soul by allowing me to use her painting of the primal wound which appears on the cover of this book.

Most of all I would like to thank my daughter's therapist Dr. Loren Pedersen, who started me on this journey into research and writing, for having the insight to understand and the ability to communicate the pain my daughter was suffering as a result of her adoption experience. His attitude of love and compassion toward all wounded people has been an inspiration to me, not only during this project, but for as long as I have known him.

And to my family, who have probably thought this book would never be finished, goes my deepest appreciation for their love, patience, and understanding.

PREFACE

This book is about adoptees. I am writing for those adoptees all over the country who have opened up their hearts to me and whose inner stories I've promised to tell. It is also written for the adoptees' birth and adoptive parents as a bridge to understanding their children and to promote the healing process for all of them. It is my hope that it will also aid professionals in their understanding of the complex issues pertaining to adoption. I will begin with my experience of what I call the *primal wound* as I observed it in my own daughter, who, twenty-three years ago, was the first person to bring it to my attention.

If anyone had told me when we brought home our three-day-old daughter on Christmas Eve, 1969, that rearing an adopted child would be different from rearing one's biological child, I, like many new and enthusiastic adoptive parents, would have laughed at them and said, "Of course it won't be different! What can a tiny baby know? We will love her and give her a wonderful home." My belief was that love would conquer all. What I discovered, however, was that it was easier for us to give her love than it was for her to accept it.

For love to be freely accepted there must be trust, and despite the love and security our daughter has been given, she has suffered the anxiety of wondering if she would again be abandoned. For her this anxiety manifested itself in typical testing-out behavior. At the same time that she tried to provoke the very rejection that she feared, there was a reaction on her part to reject us before she could be rejected by us. It seemed that allowing herself to love and be loved was too dangerous; she couldn't trust that she would not again be abandoned.

I was to discover during my ten years of research that this testing-out behavior was one of two diametrically opposed responses to having been abandoned, the other being a tendency toward acquiescence, compliance, and withdrawal. Although living with a "testing-out" child may be more difficult than living with a compliant child, I am thankful that our daughter acted in such a way so as to bring her pain to our attention. We were able, after years of trying to deal with it ourselves, to get help for her. This was the beginning of a journey which was to change all our lives.

I had no idea at the outset of her therapy that adoption had anything to do with what was going on with my daughter. Despite the fact that I had been considered a highly successful teacher, with a deep, caring, and intuitive understanding of my students, as well as the biological parent of a younger daughter who was not having these difficulties, I believed that I must somehow be at fault. For most of the acting out was directed at me, her mother. What was I doing wrong? Why was my daughter acting so hostile and angry toward me at home, yet close and loving when in public? Why was she so strong-willed and dramatic? Why did she feel the desperate need to be in complete control of every situation? Why could she not accept the love I had and wanted to give her? I have since learned that "all the hoopla is the child trying to connect with the mother," as James Mehlfeld, a therapist who works with adoptees, put it. At the same time, this attempt at bonding was sabotaged by provocative, destructive behavior on her part, as she tested and retested our love and commitment.

Because we were able to get the appropriate help for her, the outcome for us as a family did not reach the tragic proportions experienced by many adoptive families in which either the child or the parents opt out of the tense situation: The child prematurely leaves or is kicked out of the home. We have been able to see our daughter gradually emerge from an antisocial, provocative, distancing child into an outgoing, sensitive, loving young woman.

The path has not been easy. When, after three years of therapy, the preconscious feelings of rejection began to emerge into consciousness, she fought this happening as if her very life depended on it; for allowing those feelings up meant also having to feel what she perceived as her vulnerable, "defective" self, the reason for her mother's having given her up. If she could keep those feelings at bay, her integrity could be preserved and she could escape, for a while longer, annihilation. Her wound was deep, her defenses strong, and her need for understanding great.

As I sought answers to what was going on in the psyche of my own daughter, my interest began to expand to other children and their adoptive parents, many of whom seemed alienated from one another. Subsequent conversations with my daughter's therapist, Dr. Loren Pedersen, regarding the dearth of information about the effects of adoption, led to my research. The interest and encouragement shown in my research by adoptees, birthmothers, adoptive parents, and bewildered professionals convinced me to write this book.

The ideas which will be presented first came as intuitive understanding about what was going on for my own daughter. For someone who was adopted almost at birth, who was never in foster care, and who was truly wanted and loved by us, she seemed to be in a great deal of pain. As I began to observe other adoptees and their families, I became more and more convinced that adoption, which has long been considered the best solution to relinquished babies, was not the panacea that it was hoped to be. Yet it was difficult to get anyone to talk about what they were feeling, because most people had no idea what was going on.

I believed that something was going on, however, because I learned that adoptees were greatly over-represented in psychotherapy. According to 1985 statistics used by Parenting Resources of Santa Ana, California, although adoptees at that time comprised 2-3% of the population of this country, they represented 30-40% of the individuals found in residential treatment centers, juvenile hall, and special schools. They demonstrated a high incidence of juvenile delinquency, sexual promiscuity, and running away from home. They have had more difficulty in school, both academically and socially, than their non-adopted peers. The adoptees referred for treatment had relatively consistent symptoms, which are characterized as impulsive, provocative, aggressive, and antisocial.

What causes this high incidence of sociological, academic, and psychological disturbance among this population which these studies imply? What predisposes adopted children toward this vulnerability? As I sought answers to these questions, I reviewed the literature, but found something lacking in all the theories I encountered. The explanations seemed too simplistic and external. Too much was being glossed over, perhaps because as a society we have tended to ignore the exquisite awareness of infants, or perhaps because what I suspected was really going on was not easy to prove or even support with scientific data. In any case, even though many of the ideas I was reading about had validity, they left a great deal unsaid about that which I was intuiting and observing in my daughter. Was she an exception? I didn't think so. There was a kind of universality or primal quality to her pain, which didn't lend itself to simple, readily obtainable, or easily acceptable explanations.

The adoption movement began about the time I was doing my graduate work in clinical psychology. More and more adoptees were coming forth to ask for open records and to search for their lost birthmothers. I seized the opportunity and set out to interview adoptees, some of whom had searched and others who had not, to try to discover their thoughts, feelings and experiences with regard to being adopted. The result was the master's thesis upon which this book is based. I have since added the experience I have gained as a therapist working with members from all three sides of the adoption triad, as well as many, many subsequent conversations with adoptees, to ascertain what motivated their searches into their histories and into themselves.

What I discovered is what I call the *primal wound*, a wound which is physical, emotional, psychological, and spiritual, a wound which causes pain so profound as to have been described as cellular by those adoptees who allowed themselves to go that deeply into their pain. I began to understand this wound as having been caused by the separation of the child from his biological mother, the connection to whom seems mystical, mysterious, spiritual and everlasting. The implications of this discovery and the responses to it will have to inform the way we think about the importance of the mother/child relationship in the future and what we as a society are willing to do about it. Because the solutions may not be simple, ideal, or without sacrifice, I anticipate a great deal of resistance to the ideas set forth in this book. The only people who can really judge this work, however, are those about whom it is written: the adoptees themselves. Only they, as they note their responses to what is written here, will really *know* in their deepest selves the validity of this work, the existence or nonexistence of the *primal wound*.

I feel very fortunate that the relationship between my daughter and me has been such that she could communicate her pain. Some of the lessons I have had to learn on the way have been very painful to me: I have had to face the fact that I can never take the place of her birthmother. And, in concert with that, I have had to realize that neither could I take away her pain...that she would have to work it through for herself.

Are we bonded? I don't think that I would be able to write this work if we were not, but it is a bond forged in the fire of sacrifice and pain, not the easy, fluid, continuity of bonding she might have had with her birthmother. We have both suffered, but we want to create something out of that suffering. This book is an attempt to do that. Although I am doing the writing, without her I would have had neither the inspiration nor the courage to do it.

PART ONE

The Wound

> *Too often in our approach to the newborn we deal with him as if he is exactly that—"brand new." We neglect the fact that the neonate is really the culmination of an amazing experience that has lasted forty weeks. . . . By looking at the neonate as if he had "sprung full-blown from the brain of Zeus" we are missing the opportunities that the newborn's history as a fetus can provide.*
>
> —T. B. BRAZELTON

That history, to which Brazelton refers, includes the bonding in utero of the mother and child. Many doctors and psychologists now understand that bonding doesn't begin at birth, but is a continuum of physiological, psychological, and spiritual events which begin in utero and continue throughout the postnatal bonding period. When this natural evolution is interrupted by a postnatal separation from the biological mother, the resultant experience of abandonment and loss is indelibly imprinted upon the unconscious minds of these children, causing that which I call the "primal wound."

And yet, how can one prove or even support something which is preverbal, such as a wound to the psyche resulting from a trauma about which a person has no conscious memory? As a clinician, I can only infer such feelings and experiences with the help of those adoptees who allow themselves to go that far back into their pain. As a biological mother, I can know it through my own intuition and experience, a knowing which is not always observable by anyone else. At the current state of our understanding, such inferences can neither be proved nor disproved, only believed or disbelieved.

It seems to me that most authors of works on the clinical aspects of adoption, after acknowledging the fact that the child was initially abandoned by his biological mother, then ignore this as an integral part of the problems demonstrated by the child. Treatment usually focuses on the relationship between the child and his adoptive parents without truly considering the impact which the original trauma might have on the child and, hence, the family situation.

I believe that the impact of the child's trauma upon the family system is greatly underestimated by clinicians and that the focus of the dynamics is skewed to seem as if the problem resides in the parents' issues. Some of the issues which are raised by psychologists concerning the adoptive parents have to do with sexual repression, feeling rejected by the child, having an unconscious aversion toward parenthood, being over-protective, being insecure about the fact that the child is really theirs, or being unable to reconcile themselves to their infertility. Except for the last two, it is acknowledged that these same factors are not restricted to families with adopted children.

There is a great deal to look at in the histories and psyches of the adoptive parents and how these things affect their parenting of the child. Very few adoptive parents seek counseling previous to adopting, perhaps thinking that having a baby will obviate the need for such work. Yet there is certainly much work to be done. Not only do prospective adoptive parents need to examine the impact infertility has upon them, but they also need to work through their own issues of abandonment and loss in order to be able to adequately help their adopted children work through theirs. And altruistic adoptive parents, who have children already and just want to provide a family for those "poor abandoned children," need to examine their motives and expectations more closely.

Even in acknowledging all the issues which may be present for the adoptive parents, there still seems to be something which is not being recognized, an intangible something, which permeates even the best of adoptive relationships. Donovan and McIntyre pointed out that their finding has been a "striking consistency of behavior problems among adoptees whether the family is functional or dysfunctional." This, to me, indicates that there is something intrinsic in the adoptive relationship which is unique and inevitable, no matter how stable the adopting couple is to begin with. In my quest for this "intangible something," I found the adoption literature to be lacking, except by implication. No one spelled it out. Therefore, it became necessary to go beyond adoption into the realms of prenatal and perinatal psychology, bonding, abandonment, and the loss experience.

CHAPTER 1

Adoption as an Experience

The truth is, much of what we have traditionally believed about babies is false. We have misunderstood and underestimated their abilities. They are not simple beings but complex and ageless—small creatures with unexpectedly large thoughts.

— DAVID CHAMBERLAIN

The Amazing Awareness of Babies

In his book, *Babies Remember Birth*, Dr. Chamberlain goes on to say, "Babies know more than they are supposed to know. Minutes after birth, a baby can pick out his mother's face—which he has never seen—from a gallery of photos. . . . The newly discovered truth is that newborn babies have all their senses and make use of them just as the rest of us do. Their cries of pain are authentic. Babies are not unfeeling; it is *we* who have been unfeeling."

If babies remember birth, then they also remember what happened right after birth, which is that their mother, the person to whom they were connected and whom they expected to welcome them into the world, was suddenly missing. How does this experience impact the emotions and senses of a newborn baby? We can no longer assume that babies are unaware or unfeeling. There is too much evidence to the contrary, as Dr. Chamberlain has said. They feel on both the physical and emotional levels. All too often, however, neither obstetrical practices nor adoption procedures reflect this new insight.

Some of what we know isn't necessarily new but, to my knowledge, hasn't been applied to relinquished children. John Bowlby, in talking about the behavior of children who have suffered the loss of a parent through death, described the various responses a baby has to the disappearance of the mother. He claimed that the child's behavior reflects an immature attempt at mourning and is "a legitimate product of bitter experience." In my opinion, the comparison to relinquishment is valid, because for the child abandonment is a kind of death, not only of the mother, but of part of the Self, that core-being or essence of oneself which makes one feel whole.

In acknowledging this loss and its impact on all involved in adoption, there is no way one can get around the pain: the pain of separation and loss for both the child and the birthmother, and the pain of not understanding or being able to make up for that pain and loss on the part of the adoptive parents. In our society we don't like to admit the absence of absolutes or accept the idea that life is often paradoxical. Instead we deny or ignore problems for which we have no clear-cut solutions, or we polarize ourselves, both sides ignoring things obvious to the other side, as in the case of abortion. If all else fails, we anesthetize ourselves from our pain by the use of alcohol or drugs. In the case of adoption, we may deny, ignore, project, intellectualize, conceptualize, or externalize . . . anything to avoid the pain and our inability to deal with that pain.

The Need for a Permanent Caregiver

It has long been known that institutions and temporary or multiple foster care cannot adequately care for abandoned children. The lack of a permanent caregiver deprives the child of some of the requisites for normal psychological development: a continuity of relationship, emotional nurturing, and stimulation. Attachment is more difficult and bonding impossible. As the number of caregivers increases, the ability to attach diminishes and the numbing of feelings becomes more and more evident. There is often a failure to thrive and, in extreme cases, even death. What the child needs, it seems, is a permanent caregiver and the sooner the better.

Adoption, then, has been seen as the best solution to three problems: that of a biological mother who cannot, will not, or is discouraged from taking care of her child, that of the child who is then relinquished, and that of the infertile couple who want a child. The fantasy has been that the joining together of the latter two entities would produce a happy solution for everyone. The reality, however, has often been less than ideal. Despite the continuity of relationship which adoption provides, adopted children experience themselves as unwanted, are unable to trust the adoptive relationship as being permanent, and often demonstrate emotional disturbances and be-havioral problems. And, although these symptoms may be more evident in children who have had previous multiple caregivers, my research has shown that *they are also present in those children who were permanently placed at or near birth.*

This raises some interesting questions: Why is it that a child, even so young as a few hours or a few days, cannot make the transition without problems? What about those children who are never told of their adoption? Why does the substitution of parents make a dif-ference, if the adoptive parents provide a warm, caring, and loving atmosphere in which a child might grow and develop?

Adoption Issues

It has been noted by some clinicians in working with adoptees that they all have essentially the same issues whether they were adopted at birth or as teenagers. These issues center around separa-tion and loss, trust, rejection, guilt and shame, identity, intimacy, loyalty, and mastery or power and control and will be dealt with later in this book.

Although these issues may be present for all three members of the adoption triad, I will, for the most part, confine my comments to the ways in which they manifest for the adoptee. My clinical work has shown me, however, that most of these same issues are present in people who have been placed in incubators or have otherwise been separated from their mothers at birth, even though they were reunited with the original mother. The consistency of the presence of these issues among adoptees and "incubator babies" suggests that it is the experience of feeling abandoned which causes that wound.

External Considerations

In looking at ways in which to define and deal with these core issues, there are currently two popular modes of thought. One is that adoptees' problems stem from external considerations. A change in adoption laws and procedures and the unsealing of records are seen as ways to avoid the shame and insult of secrecy. More open communication between children and adoptive parents about all aspects of adoption has been recommended as a means of helping children adjust. It is certainly true that legislative changes need to be made in order to protect the civil rights of adoptees, and that an atmosphere of openness regarding adoption issues within the family will improve family dynamics, but neither of these remedies will eliminate the *primal wound.*

Independent, open adoptions have been held out as the hope of the future, because these eliminate the stigma of secrecy and lack of genealogical history and allow the adoptee and birthmother to have some kind of contact. This contact may be in the form of letters, cards, and pictures exchanged between birth and adoptive families or may include actual visits with their children by the biological relatives. I want to stress again, however, that if the birthmother is not acting as the primary caregiver, the child will suffer the loss of her in that capacity.

A relatively new suggestion has been that adoption per se be eliminated altogether and that guardianships be established instead.

This would allow the child to keep his own name and heritage and at the same time give him a permanent home. While I applaud the attempt at honesty which this idea provides, it seems to me to be a type of long-term foster care, with the child having no real sense of family at all. And none of these solutions addresses on the feeling level the question "Why am I living in this family and not with you?" Nothing can save the child from that primal pain of separation from the first mother, except keeping them together as mother and child.

One woman told me that she had intended to write a long letter to her birthmother about whom she had no conscious memory but for whom she had been thinking about searching. She wanted to explain how she felt about being adopted. She decided to write with her left hand, because she had heard that this would access her right brain and put her more in touch with her feelings. Taking pen in hand, she wrote: "Dear Mommy, Come and get me." After that, she told me, there seemed to be nothing more to say.

Adoption as a Concept

The other trend in trying to understand and eliminate the problems connected with adoption is to view them as conceptual. According to this school of thought, the problems stem from the child's being told about adoption, the idea of having two mothers, the reason for having been relinquished, and the feeling this brings up for him. In other words, it is the intellectual knowledge that he is adopted which confuses and disturbs the child. One gets the feeling from reading these ideas that adoption is only a theory, and that if we don't say too much about it, it won't have much effect. The reason we have to tell our children that they are adopted is that they might find out anyway. And then, it is best to be honest. The question shifts from *if* to *when.*

There have been and still are myriad debates about when an adoptee should be told of his adoption. Should he be told as soon as he is able to understand the word? Before? Will telling a child of his adoptive status during the very early years prolong the resolution of issues pertaining to those particular stages of personality development? Is it harmful to tell a child during those periods in his life when he might already be having conflicting feelings about his parents?

"Tell him as soon as possible, so that he will not think that it is a bad secret which has been kept from him, but will see it as a positive thing," some experts recommend. "Adoption is a complicated concept, which the child is not going to understand, so it is better to wait until he is able to comprehend what he is being told," others argue. On and on it goes.

Abandonment and Adoption as an Experience

All of this rhetoric ignores one simple but critical fact: *The adoptee was there.* The child actually experienced being left alone by the biological mother and being handed over to strangers. That he may have been only a few days or a few minutes old makes no difference. He shared a 40-week experience with a person with whom he probably bonded in utero, a person to whom he is biologically, genetically, historically and, perhaps even more importantly, psychologically, emotionally, and spiritually connected, and some people would like him to believe that it is the *telling* of the experience of the severing of that bond which makes him feel so bad!

It has been noted by parents and clinicians that many adoptees demonstrate little or no discernible reaction upon being told of their adoption. Might it not be possible this lack of reaction is a result of unconscious awareness of the fact of their adoption on the part of adoptees? Sorosky, Baran, and Pannor, in their book *The Adoption Triangle*, found this to be true, as I did in my research.

One adoptee told me about never feeling as if she belonged in her family, of not being understood. Although not told of her adoption until she was thirteen, it didn't surprise her. Another woman said, "Nobody looks like me. No one understood me." A man spoke of "a feeling of not fitting in and not knowing why." Although shocked at age 33 when finding a paper which told of his adoption, he did not feel shocked by the fact itself but by the betrayal of its having been kept from him all those years. Even though the betrayal did not fully manifest until adulthood, it had been an unconscious barrier between him and his parents throughout his childhood. There was a secret. There was something that he was not being told.

This kind of secret does little to foster trust between a child and his parents. It instead gives an air of unreality and dishonesty to the whole relationship. As pointed out by Frances Wickes in her book *The Inner World of Childhood*, there is a great deal of danger inherent in creating such an atmosphere of deception and mistrust in the life of a child. Children are primarily creatures of intuition and sensation. The world of objects is explored through sensation while they become aware of inner forces, both in themselves and others, through intuition.

In their book *Healing the Hurt Child*, Donovan and McIntyre warn parents of trying to keep secrets from their children. In an early chapter they say, ". . . we can usually demonstrate easily to the parent that the child's behavioral problems reflect an unconscious knowledge —often extremely detailed and accurate—of the supposed secret. The parent can then be shown how that unconscious knowledge plays a major role in maintaining the present disastrous situation."

Yet in a following chapter on loss in the lives of children, Donovan and McIntyre say, "The monolithic approach to adoption casework in this country dictates that the child be told about the adoption as early as possible." They go on to deride this advice by making this statement: "If the need is for knowledge, then it follows that one should inform the nonadopted child of the fact that he is 'biological.' Babies have no need to 'know' about adoption."

This extraordinary contradiction shows just how widespread is the denial of the experience suffered by adopted children. Babies already "know" about adoption. It happened to them. By keeping that knowledge unconscious, their parents deprive them of a context in which to place the feelings caused by their preconscious experience of that loss. They often feel abnormal, sick, or crazy for having those feelings and puzzled by their own behavior.

What adoptees need to know is that their experience was real. Adoption isn't a concept to be learned, a theory to be understood, or an idea to be developed. It is a real life experience about which adoptees have had and are continuing to have constant and conflicting feelings, all of which are legitimate. Their feelings are their response to the most devastating experience they are ever likely to have: the loss of their mother. Just because they do not consciously remember it does not make it any less devastating. It only makes it more difficult to deal with, because it happened before they had words with which to describe it (preverbal) and is, therefore, almost impossible to talk about. For many of them, it is even difficult to think about. In fact, some adoptees say they feel as if they either came from outer space or a file drawer. To allow themselves the memory of being born, even a feeling sense of it, would mean also having to remember and feel what happened next. And that they most certainly do not want to do.

The Importance of Early Experiences

It is understandable that adoptees might not want to remember this painful experience. But what about clinicians who don't recognize the importance of that experience? What happens when adoptees go in for therapy, and their therapist considers adoption irrelevant to their problems, even though this was part of their early experience? Psychologists often talk about the first three years of life as being the most important years in emotional development. Our current understanding of prenatal psychology has made many realize that the environment in utero is an important part of a baby's well-being. Yet, when it comes to adoption, there seems to be a black-out in awareness. There seems to be a reluctance to recognize that at the moment of birth and the next few days, weeks, or months in the life of a child, when he is separated from his mother and handed over to strangers, he could be profoundly affected by this experience. What does it mean that we have for so long wanted to ignore this?

That the child does not consciously remember it will not diminish the impact of it. How many of us remember very much about the first three years of our lives? Does our lack of memory mean that those three years have had no impact on us—our perceptions, attitudes, and behavior? How many sexually abused children remember their experiences of abuse? Are we to believe that if a person can successfully keep those experiences from consciousness, they will not affect his or her future relationships? In the case of abuse, we have now at last begun to recognize that there is, indeed, a profound lifelong effect on the person, an effect which often requires years of therapy to overcome. Yet, what if the most abusive thing which can happen to a child is that he is taken from his mother?

In her book *Necessary Losses*, Judith Viorst tells this story:

A young boy lies in a hospital bed. He is frightened and in pain. Burns cover 40 percent of his small body. Someone has doused him with alcohol and then, unimaginably, has set him on fire.

He cries for his mother.

His mother has set him on fire.

It doesn't seem to matter what kind of mother a child has lost, or how perilous it may be to dwell in her presence. It doesn't matter whether she hurts or hugs. Separation from mother is worse than being in her arms when the bombs are exploding. Separation from mother is sometimes worse than being with her when she is the bomb.

I am not suggesting that we keep a child with a mother who will set him on fire, but I am suggesting that *we have to understand what we are doing when we take him away from her.*

13

Viorst noted: "There is a time to separate from our mother. But unless we are ready to leave her and be left—anything is better than separation." Breaking that connection has a tremendous impact on the lives of both mother and child forever. This is no less true for adoptees and their biological mothers than it is for anyone else. For these babies and their mothers relinquishment and adoption are not concepts; they are experiences from which neither fully recovers.

The Trauma of Abandonment and Adoption

What the general population considers to be a concept, a social solution for the care of children who cannot or will not be taken care of by their biological parents, is really a two-part, devastating, debilitating experience for the child. The first part of the experience is the abandonment itself. No matter how much the mother wanted to keep her baby and no matter what the altruistic or intellectual reasons she had for relinquishing him or her, *the child experiences the separation as abandonment.*

The second part of the experience is that of being handed over to strangers. Even if the adoptive mother has established a relationship with the birthmother and aided in the birth of the baby, the baby will recognize her as an impostor, a substitute for the mother with whom he spent the first nine months of his life.

Dr. Chamberlain, quoted at the beginning of this chapter, and others in the field of perinatal psychology have documented evidence that babies are not the unaware, simple beings which scientists had once supposed. (Mothers, deep in their hearts, always knew this!) We now know that they are cognitive beings with a wide range of abilities, such as recognizing their own mother's face, smell, and energy, feeling a wide range of emotions, remembering, learning, and using all five senses to experience their new life outside the womb.

With all this in mind, it is easy to deduce that being handed over to a stranger must be for the baby a bewildering and even terrifying experience. Add to that the lack of physical, hormonal, psychological and emotional preparation for the adoptive mother to know the needs and be able to mirror this particular baby, and one can see that there is a great deal about which very few people seem to have given much thought.

Being handed over to someone right away is preferable, however, to being left alone in a nursery for days. I learned in talking to social workers who worked in adoption agencies that one of the ways in which these grieving babies were kept quiet was by administering phenobarbital. Being left with no one who really cares is devastating and babies scream their outrage at this denial of the basic human need to be held, to be touched. It is only recently that we have recognized this need. There is now a practice called "cuddling," in which volunteers touch or hold babies who are premature, ill, or withdrawing from narcotics. Since this program was initiated, it has been noted that babies who are touched or held recover much faster and gain more weight than babies who are denied this basic human requirement. This same consideration needs to be extended to those babies being given up for adoption.

Birthdays and Birthday Parties

My daughter told me recently that each year the three days between her birthday and the day we took her home are the three most difficult days of her life. She feels helpless, hopeless, empty, and alone. There seems to be a memory built into the psyche and cells, an anniversary reaction (also often felt by the birthmother), which sends many adoptees into despair around their birthdays.

Many clinicians and parents have told me that adoptees often act out a great deal before or during their birthday parties. They begin by having a sense of excitement, but often end up sabotaging the whole affair. "I just don't know what would get into her," one mother lamented. "Every year we would go to a great deal of trouble to have a wonderful party, yet she would act angry and resentful."

Yet is it any wonder that many adoptees sabotage their birthday parties? Why would one want to celebrate the day they were separated from their mothers? The adoptees, of course, have probably never really understood, themselves, why they do this. An adoptee said, "I don't know why I acted the way I did. I know that my mother was really trying . . . that she really wanted me to have a good time. But . . . I don't know . . . I just felt so sad and angry all at the same time. I couldn't enjoy myself. I just wanted to run away and hide." For adoptees birthdays commemorate an experience, not of joy, but one of loss and sorrow.

Summary

Adoption, considered by many to be merely a concept, is, in fact, a traumatic experience for the adoptee. It begins with the separation from his biological mother and ends with his living with strangers. Most of his life he may have denied or repressed his feelings about this experience, having had no sense that they would be acknowledged or validated. He may, instead, have been made to feel as if he should be grateful for this monumental manipulation of his destiny. Somewhere within him, however, he does have feelings about this traumatic experience, and having these feelings does not mean that he is abnormal, sick, or crazy. It means that he is wounded as a result of having suffered a devastating loss and that his feelings about this are legitimate and need to be acknowledged, rather than ignored or challenged.

CHAPTER 2

The Connection with the Birthmother

It is my thesis that in the earliest phase, we are dealing with a very special state of the mother, a psychological condition which deserves a name, such as Primary Maternal Preoccupation. . . . The mother who develops this state . . . provides a setting for the infant's constitution to begin to make itself evident, for the developmental tendencies to start to unfold. . . . There is something about the mother of a baby, something which makes her particularly suited to the protection of her infant in this state of vulnerability and which makes her able to contribute positively to the baby's positive needs.

—DONALD WINNICOTT

Donald Winnicott has done much to contribute to the understanding of the profound connection between mother and child. He has even stated that at the beginning of life there is no such thing as a baby. There is instead a mother/baby—an emotional, psychological, spiritual unit, whose knowing comes from intuition. The baby and the mother, although separated physiologically, are still psychologically one. Needless to say, such an idea has tremendous importance for the infant taken from his mother at or soon after birth.

The Mysterious Link between Mother and Child

"There is a big empty hole inside me, and I need to plug it back up. That would be my birthmother." The adoptee who said this was voicing what many adoptees have told me: No matter how close they are to their adoptive parents, there is a space reserved for the mother who gave them birth. There appears to be more to the biological connection than curiosity or a need for information.

When asked why they want to search for birth parents, adoptees will often give a socially acceptable answer, such as wanting health information or having an interest in genealogy. Yet when I asked a more specific question: "For which parent would you search, if you had to make a choice?" the majority answered, "The mother." The reason has something to do with feeling an unconscious connection with that lost mother which seems profound to them.

When asked why she would look for her mother instead of her father, Valerie said, "Somehow there is a much more powerful connection with her." Jennifer's response was, "Oh, he was just someone who loved her. She was the one I was connected to." When I asked Barbara how she happened to see my newspaper ad (asking for volunteers for my research), she answered, "Oh, I always read them. I keep hoping that someday there will be an ad from a woman asking to meet someone born on July 2, 1955, in Omaha, Nebraska."

Perhaps the most poignant testimony about this need to reconnect with the lost mother was given by Sandra, who said,

> I think it would be interesting . . . at the same time terrifying. There
> is that fear of rejection! I'm torn between a rock and a hard place.
> I would search for my mother, though. I don't understand why,
> because I've always thought it would be interesting to find out if my
> father really was artistic. Did he do that for a career? And then I
> could see definitely where I inherited my artistic ability. I think it
> would be fascinating. But I don't know . . . there's that pull back to
> the mother bit. The father is much more an intellectual thing, and

the mother is emotional. Hmmmmm, I'd never thought of that . . . very interesting . . . (and she began to cry).

Mother vs. Primary Caregiver

It is curious that seldom in psychiatric literature, so far as I have been able to determine, is there any differentiation made between *mother* and *primary caregiver*. Often it is even pointed out by an author that when using the term "mother," he is actually referring to any mother-figure, who acts as the primary caregiver. In other words, it is implied that the mother could be replaced by another "primary caregiver" with the child's being none the wiser.

I don't believe it is possible to sever the tie with the biological mother and replace her with another primary caregiver, no matter how warm, caring, and motivated she may be, without psychological consequences for the child (and the mother). An infant or child can certainly attach to another caregiver, but the quality of that attachment may be different from that with the first mother, and bonding may be difficult or, as many adoptees have told me, impossible.

Attachment and Bonding

Perhaps this would be a good place to stress the difference between *attachment* and *bonding*, as I see it, because here again are two terms which are often used interchangeably. I believe that it would be safe to say that most adopted children form attachments to their adoptive mothers. This is a kind of emotional dependence, which may seem crucial to their survival. Bonding, on the other hand, may not be so easily achieved. It implies a profound connection, which is experienced at all levels of human awareness. In the earliest stages of an infant's life, this bond instills the child with a sense of well-being and wholeness necessary to healthy emotional development. The significance of this very important beginning of life is now being stressed by many experts in the fields of obstetrics and psychology. The question as to whether

19

or not an adoptee is at a disadvantage as a result of missing the earliest imprinting or bonding experience has been raised by many professionals.

Winnicott, as the above quotation indicates, believed that the biological mother is specially prepared through that bonding to meet the needs of the child, which are communicated through intuition and other phenomena, unobservable to anyone else. There is just a *knowing* what the baby needs. Unfortunately, too many mothers do not or cannot (because of work or other distractions) tune in to these unconscious signals and instead rely upon "experts" to tell them what to do. Experts can't really help, however, because it isn't just a matter of knowing how to care for a baby, but what this particular baby needs at this particular time.

It seems as if a mother may be biologically, hormonally, and emotionally programmed to bond and respond to her baby at birth in the same way that she was able to do when the fetus was in the womb. There are a series of sensations and events, some of which begin in utero, which aid in the postnatal bonding experience: breast-feeding, odors, eye contact, touching, and familiar sounds, such as the heartbeat and voice. That a baby knows its own mother at birth has been proven over and over.

Some psychologists believe these events to be stage-specific, which means that if they are delayed, as in the case of a newborn separated from his mother, both mother and child will experience grief. An adoptive mother may be at a disadvantage in coping with the affective behavior of her child, for she doesn't understand the form or depth of his grief or the limitations placed upon her as his mother. The infant has missed something which cannot be replaced even by the most motivated of adoptive mothers.

The Broken Bond

What the child has missed is the security and serenity of oneness with the person who gave birth to him, a continuum of bonding from prenatal to postnatal life. This is a profound connection for which the adoptee forever yearns. It is this yearning which leaves him often feeling hopeless, helpless, empty, and alone. In working with adoptees, it is apparent that no matter what happens a month, a year, or several years in the future, that period immediately after birth, when the infant has made the transition from the warm, fluid, dark security of the womb to the cold, bright, alien world of postnatal life, is a crucial period. It is a time when a baby needs to be in proximity to his mother in order to find the world safe and welcoming instead of confusing, uncaring, and hostile. At that time the mother is the whole world for the baby, and his connection to her is essential to his sense of well-being and wholeness.

It is my belief, therefore, that *the severing of that connection between the adopted child and his birthmother causes a primal or narcissistic wound, which affects the adoptee's sense of Self and often manifests in a sense of loss, basic mistrust, anxiety and depression, emotional and/or behavioral problems, and difficulties in relationships with significant others.* I further believe that the awareness, whether conscious or unconscious, that the original separation was the result of a "choice" made by the mother affects the adoptee's self-esteem and self-worth.

"I Want My Mommy"

It is believed by some psychologists that children up to the age of two or three years can sometimes remember their birth and subsequent events, but that after age 2 1/2 or 3 those memories fade, to be brought up to consciousness only through hypnosis. In any event there have been reports made to me by adoptive mothers that upon hearing their toddlers crying at night they have been unable to comfort them and have been told, "I want my mommy." One mother said that when she assured her daughter that "Mommy's right here," she was told, "I want my other mommy," a mommy from whom she was separated at birth.

I can recall a similar experience with my own child. She did not often cry at night, but the few times that she did, although she didn't say anything, she would not let me hold or comfort her. Now I know that I was not the person who *could* comfort her. A more insightful mother said to her son, under similar circumstances, "You miss her don't you, Todd?" That kind of acknowledgment of feelings goes a long way toward establishing trust between adoptive mother and child. In most cases, in our ignorance, we just feel rejected ourselves and helpless to comfort a grieving baby.

Birthmother Fantasies

Even if they have no conscious memories of her, many adoptees have fantasies about their birthmothers. Some also have fantasies about birthfathers and siblings. Anna, who was relinquished at age two, talked about having a feeling sense of being in her birthmother's arms, although she couldn't actually remember her. She has had many fantasies about her and used to talk to her. She also used to cry for her, yet said that she couldn't understand why she would cry "for someone I never knew."

Diane, another adoptee who has had many fantasies about her birthmother, created a second identity for herself in which she gave herself the name Jennifer. She felt this identity to be somehow connected to her birthmother. She said that she could be more herself during the times when she was being Jennifer, because "I was not being the Diane of my adoptive parents' creation. She (Jennifer) had to be a secret, though. My parents wouldn't have liked her." Whether or not her adoptive parents would have liked "Jennifer" may never be known, but it was Diane's perception that they would not.

Ralph talked of having "fairy-godmother" fantasies about his birthmother. She was a wonderful mother, who would eventually come back to claim him. She would intuitively know what he wanted or needed and would always be good to him. Some men, in an attempt to duplicate or recreate the experience of the all-knowing mother, try to turn their wives into mind-reading mothers who can anticipate their every need. The wish is understandable, but in reality the only person who might have been able to intuit his every need without any effort on his part to make those needs known would have been (as in Ralph's fantasy) the birthmother, and then only for the first few months of his life.

Carol said that as a child she had completely repressed any fantasies about her birthmother. Recently, however, she has done some group work concerning her feelings of having been given up for adoption. During one of the sessions in which she was visualizing her relinquishment, she cried out, "No, don't give me up! Don't give me away." She said that she doesn't know how accurate the verbalizing might be, since the experience was preverbal, but the feelings were very powerful.

Joan, who was adopted at age four, admitted to having some fantasies at first, but as she got older she forgot what her first mother looked like and almost ceased thinking about her. "A child is too busy to think about those things. I don't remember thinking much about it growing up." This is a woman for whom denial has been such a valuable defense. It has protected her from her feelings about her birthfather's putting her in an orphanage at age four as well as her adoptive father's verbal and sexual abuse. "Strange thing! None of this bothered me." She claimed to have had no depression or anxiety, no fears, no identity conflicts, and no problems in relationships. "I feel very fortunate that I have no scars like you hear people talking about." Yet she did begin to stutter shortly after having been adopted and those who know her best say that she can get only "so close" to people.

Stephanie didn't have any fantasies until a few years ago, when she began to have quite specific images. She said that she had the feeling, around Thanksgiving and Christmas, that she should be in a house with a lot of people. She believed that she should be in a certain house, which she could visualize, talking to her brothers and sisters. She had very strong feelings around the holidays. She has, since that first interview, found her birthmother, who still lives in the state in which Stephanie was born. She has also found many relatives, some of whom live within a few miles of her present home. Now holidays are, as in her fantasies (memories?), large, joyous, family gatherings!

George, rather than fantasizing about his birthmother, fantasized about having a twin brother. He said that it wasn't just that he was lonely and needed a phantom playmate, but a real feeling that "there was once another one like me." One might wonder if he has a twin from whom he was separated at birth.

Barbara was another adoptee who fantasized about a sibling. She daydreamed about having a sister whom she called Anna. This sister was going to rescue her (although from what, she couldn't say). She and her neighbor would endlessly play a game which they called "The Princess and the Slave Girl." Barbara was a damsel in distress waiting to be rescued. "I'm being tortured or in prison and someone has to come and rescue me," usually her "sister." Of the game she said, "It wasn't so much a fairy tale as kind of how I felt." She felt that something was being worked out with this game.

The feeling of needing to be rescued is a theme which comes up quite frequently in my conversations with adoptees. Ken said that he always had the feeling that someday someone was going to come and rescue him from his situation, although he didn't consider his situation to be very bad. It later seemed to him that it was a wish to be relieved from anxiety—that his birthmother could do that. Even though his early fantasies about his birthmother were positive, the idea of someone taking him away from his adoptive family filled him with another kind of anxiety.

Not all fantasies about the mother are positive. Debbie's fantasy was that her birthmother "is hard pressed for a better life and leaves me. My birthfather is wealthy and kind and finds me and pays all my bills." One day, while riding on rapid transit, she said that she "freaked out" when a companion pointed out another woman who looked like her and said, "She could be your mother." Debbie felt panicky and moved to another car of the train.

Carrie, who did not fantasize until she began to search, has also had negative feelings about her mother. She had been afraid that her mother wouldn't want to see her, wouldn't care about her, would hang up the phone without talking to her, and would consider her an intruder. She has since located her birth family and has met everyone except her mother. Everyone has been very accepting of her. But the one person who really counts doesn't want to see her. Although the fear of a second rejection by the birthmother is common among searching adoptees, Carrie feels as if there might have been something in her mother's attitude while pregnant with her that made her think that she wouldn't be welcome. Regardless of whether or not the initial rejection took place before or after birth, being rejected for the second time is devastating for the adoptee.

The Difference Between Understanding and Feeling

Many people believe that carefully explaining to the adoptee the reasons for his relinquishment will alleviate the pain of that experience. It is certainly understandable that a birthmother would want her child to know her reasons for surrendering. Yet I maintain that the child will *feel* rejected and abandoned nevertheless. An example from my own experience will help to make this clear: One night my daughter, who was 14 at the time, was talking to me about her feelings toward her birthmother. She said, "I *understand* that she had to give me up, Mom, but why doesn't that make me *feel* any better?" I replied, "It is the 14-year-old girl who understands the reasons for her relinquishment, but the *feelings* are those of a newborn baby who simply feels the loss of a mother who never came back." The baby doesn't care *why* she did it; the baby just feels abandoned. *And that abandoned baby lives inside each and every adoptee all his or her life.*

25

Confusion Between Love and Abandonment

Although understanding the reasons for certain experiences in life is interesting and sometimes even helpful, reasons are for adults, not babies. I have heard of adoptive mothers who, when a child expresses anger at the birthmother, will say, "Oh, you shouldn't feel that way; after all, she loved you and did what she thought was best for you." The idea that the birthmother loved the baby so much that she gave him away is a non sequitur so far as the child is concerned. There is an equation here: love = abandonment. This may contribute to the fear of connecting to the adoptive mother, since allowing oneself to love and be loved may be associated with subsequently being abandoned.

This is not to say that explanations should not be given if the adoptive parents have that information. The adoptee has the right to all available information about himself. Questions about the relinquishment, however, are tricky for adoptive parents to handle. On the one hand they want to impart to the child that his birthmother was trying to do her best for him, while at the same time they don't want him to fear another abandonment. Adoptive parents are often guessing when it comes to others' motives, and they would probably do better by being honest about their lack of information concerning the relinquishment. And even if they do know why the birthmother relinquished, it would be presumptuous to believe that this information would take away the pain of having been given up. Thinking and feeling are two different things. Both are important and need to be acknowledged, respected, and honored.

Summary

The connection between a child and his biological mother appears to be primal, mystical, mysterious, and everlasting. It can no longer be assumed that one can replace the biological mother with another "primary caregiver" without the child's being both aware of the substitution and traumatized by it. The mother/infant bond takes many forms and the communication between them is unconscious, instinctual, and intuitive. To those researchers who want to believe only what they can observe, this may not seem very scientific. It is understood by mothers, however, to whom it does not seem to be all that mysterious. The significance of that bond is confirmed by the increasing numbers of adoptees and birthmothers who are out there searching for one another.

Although the idea of searching to reconnect with the biological mother is filled with conflict and anxiety, it should not be regarded as pathological. It should, in fact, be regarded as healthy. We all need the biological, historical, emotional, and existential connection which is denied so many adoptees. For them, searching might be seen as an attempt to heal the primal wound about which there are no conscious thoughts, only feelings and somatic memories—and an aching sense of loss.

CHAPTER 3

The Loss of the Mother
and The Sense of Self

*The biological birth of the human infant and the
psychological birth of the individual are not coin-
cident in time. The former is a dramatic, observable, and well-circumscribed event; the latter a
slowly unfolding intrapsychic process.*

    —MAHLER, PINE, & BERGMAN

What is it which causes such a devastating wound to the psyches
of children separated from their biological mothers? Mahler, Pine, and
Bergman, quoted above, subscribe to the idea that physical birth and
psychological birth do not happen simultaneously and that for several
months after physical birth takes place, the infant remains psychologically merged with the mother.

The phenomenon of physical birth can be readily observed and
documented. The "slowly unfolding intrapsychic process" of
psychological birth, on the other hand, proceeds largely unnoticed by
anyone other than the mother and child themselves. The infant, as
he matures in the first year of life, gradually begins to experience
himself as being separate from his mother, rather than as an extension
of her. The mother, then, becomes a love object for the child, the
source of his security and of the satisfaction of his needs. The
significance of this process to the child's feeling of well-being should
alert us to the havoc which may be wrought should this tie be
prematurely severed and the continuum of bonding interrupted.

Dual Unity with the Mother

Eric Neumann expresses a similar idea and reminds us that the human child requires a period of a year after birth, which he calls the "extra-uterine embryonic phase," to attain the degree of maturity that characterizes the young of most other mammals at birth. During this time, though the physical body is already born, the Self or core-being of the infant is not yet separate from that of the mother but psychologically is contained within her. The nature of the relationship between mother and child is characterized, not by subject and object, but by a kind of fluidity of being, of mother/child/world transcending both time and space. The mother provides a container for the child's developing ego, just as she had previously provided the container for his developing physical body.

Both Mahler and Neumann describe this relationship as dual unity in which the mother not only acts as the child's Self, but actually is that Self. An uninterrupted continuum of being within the matrix of the mother is necessary in order for the infant to experience a rightness or wholeness of self from which to begin his separation or individuation process. The continuity and quality of this primal relationship is crucial, because it may set the tone for all subsequent relationships.

A Break in the Continuum of Bonding

Relinquishment and adoption is not the only case where the psychobiological continuum is interrupted. Babies separated during war and other disasters, premature infants who are placed in incubators, and even babies who are the victims of modern obstetrical practices (where mothers are kept in one room of the hospital and the babies in another) may suffer from this interruption of the continuum of primal relationship to the mother. Being returned to the biological mother may be better for the child than being handed over to someone else, but there still may be a lack of trust in the continuity of the goodness and rightness of his environment and of himself.

One might metaphorically think of the discontinuity of the mother/child unit as the breaking of a plate. If one breaks a plate then glues it back together, although there should be a good "fit" because the same pieces are used, there is now glue separating the two parts. Let us assume that this glue symbolizes a tenuous bond that cannot be trusted as being as strong as the original whole plate. There may always be a feeling that the plate can again be broken, that separation can reoccur.

In the case of adoption, not only does the plate have to be glued back together, but the other half of the plate is different, so that the pieces will not quite fit together. There is always a feeling of "not fitting." Not only is there less trust in the strength of the bonding, the glue, but that bonding is made even more tenuous by the poor fit between the two pieces. Some pieces may fit better than others, but only the original is that other half. For the child who has experienced these "breaks" in the continuity of bonding, his trust in the environment has been shaken and his sense of Self has been compromised. Something is broken; something is missing, and it will never be the same again.

Premature Ego Development

In addressing the sense of Self, Daniel Stern's ideas differ from those of Mahler and of Neumann. Stern does not believe that the infant begins life merged with the mother, but that he is separate and has a sense of this separateness right from the beginning. He maintains that to be merged implies a previous separation, and while semantically Stern may be correct, I agree with Mahler that, under ideal conditions, the infant is psychologically still part of the maternal matrix (perhaps *not yet emerged*, rather than merged.) She is his whole environment, his whole world. If for some reason the mother cannot be counted on to be the "whole environment" for the infant, he begins to take over that function from her. Rather than a gradual, well-timed developmental process, the child is forced by this wrenching

30

experience of premature separation to be a separate being, to form a separate ego before he should have to do so. This phenomenon is often referred to as "premature ego development" and is sometimes considered to be pathological. This is not to say that there might not be some advantages to premature ego development. It may provide survival value. Indeed, because adoptees often find the world hostile, this aspect of premature ego development is often felt as that which saves them from annihilation.

Although this "survival-value" aspect of premature ego development may become unnecessary when the child is placed with the adoptive parents, he does not perceive this. His experience is that the protector may at any time disappear. Rather than trusting the permanence of the caregiver, many adoptees never feel as if they can count on anyone; they have to be self-sufficient in life. Their feelings about this go as far back as they can remember—and probably farther. Paula, in trying to put words to these feelings, said, "It was as if I figuratively sat up in my crib and said to myself, 'I can't trust anyone. I will have to take care of myself.'"

The danger, so far as our considerations are concerned, is that we may too readily accept this premature ego development as proof that the child is adjusting well to his environment. Although in a sense this is true, we have to keep in mind that in having been separated from his mother, the child has found the environment to be hostile. He should not have had to make this adjustment at so young an age, but should have been allowed to bask for a while longer in paradise. Whereas labeling premature ego development as pathological may be extreme, we should not ignore the importance of timing and sequence in the developmental processes. For this reason, I believe that an accelerated maturation process is inappropriate at this particular stage of development, with consequences which I shall enumerate later.

There are other reasons to support the concept that a child's developing a sense of Self is more gradual than Stern would have us believe, and that the dual unity with the mother might be the more

31

natural and desired state. One reason comes from my own experience as a mother. Having given birth as well as having adopted, I know that there are many things which happen between mother and infant which are intuitive and unobservable, yet real and significant to the mother/child bond and the communication between them. It is the kind of unconscious, instinctive relationship which Neumann has called the "participation mystique." During this beginning phase in the baby's life, when a non-verbal, intuitive, and unconscious communication takes place between mother and child, is it not possible that the biological mother may be irreplaceable by anyone else? She may be, as Winnicott and others have described, uniquely prepared for this role.

The second reason for my believing in the early "dual unity" between mother and child comes from the testimony of adoptees. They tell me that they feel as if part of themselves (or their Selves) is missing, a phenomenon they sometimes describe as "phantom limb pain"—a sense of something missing. So long as a child's ego remains embedded within the matrix of the mother, he is free of the threat of the loss of Self. However, if a child is separated from her before gaining a sense of Self separate from her, he may feel incomplete.

The Ideal State of the Self

If, indeed, Stern is right that all infants have a separate sense of Self right from birth, perhaps it is the "ideal state of the Self" which is injured in the separation from the mother. What is this "ideal state of the Self" and how might it relate to the way in which a relinquished child responds to the world? It is thought by many psychologists that this ideal state is a feeling of rightness, well-being, and wholeness, which reflects a harmonious atmosphere of safety and security from which a child can develop a strong sense of self-esteem. It is a state of primary narcissism considered appropriate to this stage of life. The opposites of this state are the feelings of anxiety, sorrow, and loneliness. One source of these feelings is the separation of an infant from his mother. These are the feelings most often described by those adoptees who have at last ceased to deny or repress their feelings.

Once these feelings surface, there is often an accompanying urge to search for the birthmother as a source of relief from that pain. There is a yearning to return to that state of well-being which lies embedded in the emotional, cellular, and, perhaps, spiritual memory of adoptees. The tie to the mother and the apparent need to reconnect with her, then, is not only a longing to find the lost object, but a longing to find the lost Self.

The Search for the Self

The search for Self is a mission for many adoptees who believe that their "baby soul" was annihilated upon the separation from the original mother. The search for Self, therefore, seems to be intimately connected to the search for the birthmother. "Trying to find my mother is connected to trying to find my sense of self," is how Erica put it. Paul described it this way: "I feel as if I'll never know who I am until I find her (birthmother). It isn't just a genetic thing. It's *who I am*—more like the soul, my real self." Janet said, "It has something to do with finding out about myself, and it has something to do with trying to explain to myself what happened. I want to know why." Gerald said, "Even though I was an adult before I found out that I was adopted, I have always felt incomplete, as if something got lost between the hospital and home—or maybe even before that. I don't know if finding my real mother will make me more complete, but I have to try it. I have to do something!"

The False Self

Perhaps the strength of this primal relationship has been underestimated because of the apparent adjustment many children make to the new environment. As adults we believe what we want to believe, and we want to believe that a child who is not causing any trouble is well-adjusted. It is important that parents not be lulled into believing that this child suffers no pain—that "my child is not having those problems." Adjustment often means shutting down—creating a "false self."

What is the false self and how does it manifest? Many adoptees I've treated, most of whom did not act out in childhood, speak of having a sense that the baby they were died, and that the one that they "decided" to become was going to have to be different, to be better, so that he would not once again be abandoned. They became people pleasers, constantly seeking approval. As children, they were very cooperative, polite, charming, and generally good. But locked inside them is pain and the fear that the unacceptable baby who "died" will come back to life if they are not vigilant. They can never truly bond with anyone, because they are not being themselves. They relate an inability to show how they feel about things, especially the so-called negative feelings of anger, hostility, disappointment, or sorrow. With the compliant adoptee, the problem is what *isn't* happening, rather than what is. The tendency toward a false self is important to recognize as a defensive coping mechanism and deserves further investigation, because it is often seen as a good adjustment with the child being given no opportunities to truly be himself.

Even with all this energy-consuming work of creating a "good" false self, most adoptees perceive themselves to be not only less than ideal, but defective or "bad." Beth who is in fact charming, beautiful, and very talented, describes herself as a "rotten, crummy, unworthy person." Although most adoptees are not so vehement in their denunciations of themselves, they nevertheless often voice apprehension about allowing anyone to see the "real" person beneath the mask.

As Patty put it, "I don't want people to know how insecure I feel. Not letting people know keeps me more in control." Jed said that he was always secretive about his feelings, believing them to be dangerous. Janice, who says that it is much easier for her to address huge crowds of people in an impersonal manner than to have a one-on-one, in-depth conversation with someone, knows that people see her as a competent, worthwhile person. She doesn't feel like that inside, however. She feels very insecure and distrusts others' motives.

Victoria uses her false self to protect herself. She said, "I'm not always sure against what, except rejection." Danielle said, "If people don't know how insecure I feel, then they wouldn't . . . couldn't get a reaction from me." Richard offered that some of the false self is necessary. "Some of that's discipline. It has to be." To others he knows that he seems in charge of himself, but inside he feels "a wreck."

Virginia gave a similar example: Many people see her as dynamic, dramatic, and extraverted, yet she feels small and lonely inside. Sometimes she is afraid that others can see what is really going on inside. She believes that she is changing, however—that healing is taking place. She said,

> It seems that I've always been who I am, but I am just starting to
> *be* who I am. I've changed a lot in the last seven years, but I don't
> think I've really changed; I've just become more myself. A changing
> is a becoming.

While it is true that most people have a social persona which they show to the world, it seems that the false self of the adoptee is more exaggerated; there is more of a feeling of discrepancy between the inside self and the outside self. Perhaps an observation from my daughter when she was 14 years old encapsulates the general feeling: "If someone rejects the outside you, that's not so bad, because it isn't really you; but if you let someone know who you really are inside and they reject you, that's *really* rejection!" The false self is the adoptees' method of adjusting to their environment in order to protect themselves from further abandonment and rejection.

Rejection and Basic Trust

Yet even the false self cannot ward off the feeling of rejection and the loss of basic trust which ensues. The sense of rejection caused by the original separation may have untold effects on the ego development of the child, as has previously been suggested. Florence Clothier suggests that besides the usual demands made upon the ego, the abandoned child must also compensate for the wound left by the loss of the biological mother. He is denied the primal relationship, the continuity of nurturing and security experienced in utero, as he makes his entrance into the new and alien world outside the womb.

The feeling that life is unsafe and that he must be "on guard" takes its toll. Part of that which might be sacrificed in ego development is a sense of spontaneity and carefree abandon, which may be associated with the early trauma of the disappearance of the mother. The loss of the mother disallows the achievement of basic trust, the first milestone in the healthy development of a human being. The ability to be spontaneous, to enjoy life, is rooted in trust that the mother will be there to keep the child safe. (Impulsivity, common among adopted children, should not be mistaken for spontaneity.)

Part of my belief that the loss of basic trust and subsequent behaviors are a result of prolonged separation from the mother is based on studies of children placed in incubators at birth. One such study by Renaldo Maduro is a case in point. Maduro studied an identical twin who had been in an incubator for several weeks following her premature birth, and who thus felt abandoned by her mother. Although she was eventually reunited with her mother, she had lost her sense of basic trust, not only in the reliability of the mother to be there, but in her own basic goodness. Many of the coping mechanisms of what Maduro called her "baby mind" were identical to what many adoptees have told me they experience. He described it this way:

- It (her baby mind) would react with bodily feelings to mental pain.

- It would substitute things for people, especially when they offered comfort, safety, and reliability.

- It would not depend on anyone else in a close way, because the "feeder" could go away or change suddenly. This includes the perfectionist need to do everything by herself without help from others.

- It would feel narcissistic depletion, emptiness inside with intense longing. This state leads to severe distress and to harmful interference with a basic loving investment of one's own body image and the development of object relations.

- It would feel in touch always with a conscious deep sadness but not necessarily depression, since in infancy the opportunity to consolidate the mother imago experience did not occur. In a sense there will never be a replacement for the lost mother . . .

- It would be prone to utilize paranoid-schizoid mechanisms of defense, because closeness is imagined to include mutual damage and destruction.

- It would turn away from life with an attitude of sour grapes, derived from strong oral envy, or to detach and turn away in apathy. . . . After protest came despair, and after despair came detachment.

- It would use depression as an attack. Since depression is a form of anger it can be used skillfully to inspire guilt and control another, but at one's own expense in the end.

- It would fear her own destructiveness . . . and (feel) intense blameworthiness.

This last point might be what is meant when adoptees refer to feeling as if they were responsible for what happened to them. It might be connected, not only to the loss of the mother, but to the loss of their own sense of goodness—their sense of Self or the "ideal state of the self."

Summary

The integrity of the Self is necessary to the healthy development of the ego and its ability to relate to others. Any injury to the basic goodness of the Self, or to what some authors refer as the "ideal state of the self," interferes with the timing and sequence of healthy ego development and results in that which I call the "primal wound."

This wound, occurring before an infant has begun to separate its own identity from that of its mother, may result in a feeling that part of oneself has disappeared, leaving the infant with a feeling of incompleteness or lack of wholeness. That incompleteness is often experienced, not only in the genealogical sense of being cut off from one's roots, but in a felt sense of bodily incompleteness.

For the child relinquished at the primal phase of development, when the mother not only plays the role of the child's Self but actually is that Self, we may be dealing not only with the loss of the "primary love object," but with the loss of part of the Self. At that primal stage, the child's inability to mourn the loss of mother or of Self and his need to guard against further loss may cause him to adopt a false self.

If the false self takes the form of an acquiescent, compliant child, the child is seen as being well-adjusted and not suffering any psychological pain. Others, however, in an attempt to demonstrate their pain and test the commitment of their parents, act out and may end up in psychiatric treatment, group homes, or jail. Neither is operating from the true Self, but from a false self and from a profound sense of loss.

CHAPTER 4

Loss and the Mourning Process

Etymologically, the word mourning means "to remember" and stems from the same root as memory. In mourning we are held in the memory of what has been lost or abandoned until we have found a replacement for it. Mourning occurs whether we have ever experienced actual death or not. Mourning and depression are the other names of abandonment.

—GILDA FRANTZ

The Need to Mourn

The infant's memory of the biological mother has not been understood by most social workers or adoptive parents. Little has been written about the consequences which might ensue as a result of the original separation from the biological mother. It has been assumed that any deprivation which might have occurred could be overcome by the adoptive parents. Many adoptive parents are still operating from the same ignorance that we did when we adopted our daughter: "What does a tiny baby know?" That an adopted child would grieve has not been adequately addressed in the literature. Yet for a child, absence and death may amount to the same thing, and the memory of the loss of the original mother may be imprinted in his psyche and cells. Although the baby cannot communicate this memory to the adoptive mother (or if he does, she fails to comprehend it), it is best to assume that he is in a state of grief. His need to attach should not cloud one's understanding of this. The loss is real and the need for mourning acute.

The Unacknowledged Attempt to Grieve

The child's experience of the loss of the biological mother may be the precipitating factor which disposes adoptees to emotional disturbance. In the relationship between mother and infant, after all, it is the mother's role to prevent the occurrence of traumatic events which might hinder normal psychological development. The birthmother's failure to prevent, and, in fact, inadvertently to cause, this traumatic state may set the stage for the child's future failures to successfully integrate events pertaining to separation and loss. Because few adoptive parents realize that their baby is experiencing loss, they do nothing to acknowledge that loss or empathize with it. Yet it is possible that much of that which constitutes pathology in adopted children, such as depression, anxiety, and oppositional disorder, could be interpreted as an attempt to deal with that loss.

For those children adopted during the first two or three years of life, whose conscious memories do not include that initial separation, the ability to deal with subsequent losses may be greatly hindered. In any case, the inability of the baby to deal with his loss, the tendency of the child to fantasize about his birthmother, and the compulsion for many adult adoptees to reconnect with the biological mother are normal responses to the severing of that first connection and should not be seen as pathological.

The Stages of Grief

The severing of that connection initiates a grieving process for both mother and child. Babies who are separated from their mothers demonstrate several stages of grief, which correspond to those seen in adults but are more difficult to discern. The initial response is one of protest and an urgent effort to recover the lost mother. According to some social workers who worked at adoption agencies, this is the stage at which babies have been administered phenobarbital in order to quiet the anguish and rage as they cry for their missing mothers.

Next comes despair. Although there is still a longing for the lost mother, the hope of being reunited with her diminishes. The child stops crying and, instead, becomes withdrawn, depressed, and detached. If, after the loss, the child is put into the consistent care of another mother-figure, he will be aloof and distant with her for some time, but will eventually attach to her. There is still a difference, however, between the attachment the child will make to the adoptive mother and that with the first mother. John Bowlby, in his monumental trilogy on separation and loss, puts it this way: "Provided there is one particular mother-figure to whom he can relate and who mothers him lovingly he will in time take to her and treat her almost as though she were his mother." That "almost" is the feeling expressed by some adoptive mothers, who feel as if they had accepted the infant as their child, but that the child had not accepted them as mother. The aloofness or lack of response to affection is often felt by the mother as rejection, yet it is the result of an important defensive process in the child as a part of mourning. He is defending against vulnerability and further loss.

Defending Against Further Loss

This response was demonstrated by Janice, who volunteered to undergo regressive hypnosis in order to reexperience her birth and adoption. The results surprised her, for, although she saw her relationship with her adoptive mother as negative, until doing this experiment she never considered the part she may have played in making the relationship difficult. She discovered that as an infant she did not want anything to do with her adoptive mother, but instead wanted to be left alone. This was corroborated by her mother's memories of their meeting. It also corresponds to my first meeting with my daughter, where she cried when I held her for the first time. (She had not yet reached the stage of detachment in her grieving process, but was still protesting.)

It had never occurred to Janice that her adoptive mother needed to feel accepted by her and that she may have, instead, felt rejected; yet it seemed to fit with her own feelings and with what her mother had told her. This is not to say that as a baby Janice could have acted any differently (after all, she was being handed over to a stranger and her behavior was appropriate to the confusing and even terrifying experience it must have been for her). It is interesting to consider, though, that adoptees may not realize the impact that they had on their adoptive parents at the beginning of their lives. It might be helpful for the parents to understand the reasons for their feelings of being rejected in order to respond sensitively to the child. Those mothers whose babies have already become detached probably will not notice that they are being experienced as the wrong mother.

Even after the child has become attached to the new mother, the experience which happens to adopted children and those who have suffered the loss of a parent through death appears to be similar: There is a fear of further loss, the loss of another parent either by death or desertion. This may be manifested as separation anxiety, but is often mistaken for a strong attachment. An example of this was expressed by an adoptee named Anthony, who says that he reacts very poorly to long-term separations and always felt that being sent to camp was his parents way of "getting rid" of him. He was afraid that they would not be there when he returned. Separation anxiety is common among adopted children.

Joe, whose father died when he was seven, says that he has a terrible time with separation and loss. He doesn't go to airports to see people off if they mean anything to him. "I hate goodbyes!" Melinda, who says that she has more difficulty with long-term separations than with death, has gotten "physically and mentally sick" at three-week separations from her husband. She attributes this to missing "my best friend to talk with," but such a severe reaction would seem to go deeper than that.

Psychosomatic Response to Loss

Although I did not specifically ask about it in the interviews, many adoptees spontaneously mentioned having some kind of chronic illness as children, which often persisted into adulthood. The symptoms mentioned included stomach aches, chronic headaches or migraines, allergies or asthma, chronic fatigue, immune deficiencies, eczema or hives, tics, and stuttering.

Bill, who suffered from allergies, developed an allergic reaction to something new each time he began to find relief with the use of antigens. Joanne had chronic diarrhea until age twenty, when she began therapy. This was similar to the experience of Valerie, who had been troubled by asthma and stomach aches, and who also found relief during the course of therapy.

Stephanie had stomach aches and headaches as a child and also suffered from severe homesickness. The symptoms would be worst when she was away from her mother. She would become panicky and get "that horrible feeling in your stomach," even from short separations from her mother. She called her mother several times while on her honeymoon, yet she wasn't really able to talk with her when she was with her.

The most-reported chronic somatic or physical disorder was stomach aches. This makes sense when one realizes the close association between gastrointestinal functioning and emotional states. These relationships have been noticed throughout history and are reflected in the folk language by expressions such as "not being able to stomach" something, noting that some situation "makes me sick," or being "fed up" with a situation. All of these responses may be seen as a result of anxiety, an anxiety which, for adoptees, may be caused by the unconscious fear of another abandonment and the deprivation of food or nurturing.

If a person is conscious of the nature of a dangerous situation, he reacts with fear and his gastric activity shuts down. He can respond to the danger by either fighting or fleeing. But if a person, like the adoptee, has no conscious memory of the source of that fear (the fear of abandonment), he may experience that fear as free-floating anxiety in which gastric activity works overtime. The resulting pain or illness is different from hypochondria, in which the symptoms are imagined. *These ill-nesses are real*, but the cause is psychological, rather than organic.

In my research, adoptees who acted out had fewer physical symptoms than those who were compliant. This makes sense, since neurotic be-havior seems to relieve the need for a somatic response. Anxiety is seen as evidence of the lack of serious psychological disintegration. If the conflict continues to be impossible to resolve, as in the case of the child who cannot be reunited with his birthmother, for instance, symptomatic changes may relieve the strain of conflict. In other words, the illness may be a way of containing or structuring the anxiety. As such, it may be protecting the adoptee against a greater harm.

I have noticed in both my research and clinical work that the experiences of loss in the earliest days of life may leave some people with somatic (bodily or physical) memory traces, which get triggered by later experiences. Many adoptees have reported to me that they were told that they vomited a great deal during the early days of their lives in their adoptive families. Some of the adoptees reported that later, as toddlers, they suffered from stomach aches when separated from their adoptive mothers. As adults, some adoptees had stomach pains when separated from their spouses. These symptoms might qualify as reawakenings of somatic memory traces. In working with regressed patients in therapy, a pain so deep that it is felt as cellular is sometimes triggered. For the many adoptees who reported having stomach aches and other illnesses as children and even as adults, this may have been a way for them to organize their anxiety in such a way as to prevent its more severe emotional manifestations.

Basic Fault

Another result of the separation of the child from the first mother may be a sense that he causes this separation himself. Not only is there a sense that he might have contributed to whatever caused the loss, but that he is "bad" as a result of it. This may be especially true for adoptees who, because they feel unwanted by their birthmothers, blame themselves for not having been good enough to keep. The intellectual reason for his relinquishment does not seem to eliminate the adoptee's feelings about it.

At the same time that the adoptee may feel at fault for what happened, he may also feel as if the birthmother "did it" to him. There is a paradoxical feeling of "I did it; you did it to me" going on, which confuses not only the adoptee himself, but everyone else, too. Resentment and rage against the lost parent are connected to feelings of shame and guilt, to which the child may respond with aggressive and destructive outbursts toward the adoptive parents. Not understanding the dynamics of the situation, adoptive parents often react with insensitivity and rejection, instead of acknowledgment and understanding.

On the other hand, rather than subjecting themselves to the pain of believing that their birthmothers didn't want them, some adoptees blame their adoptive parents for having stolen them. They feel confused and conflictual as a result of wanting and waiting to be rescued, while at the same time fearing the separation from the only parents they have consciously known. This inner conflict causes a great deal of behavioral problems between adoptees and their adoptive parents. On the other hand, some children, in an effort to avoid a further abandonment, may adopt an attitude of compliance and acquiescence, withdrawing and behaving the way they perceive their parents want them to behave.

The Death of the Psyche

Sometimes the sense of loss experienced by adoptees becomes so overwhelming that it leads to thoughts of suicide. These feelings are characterized by hopelessness, helplessness, emptiness, and loneliness—feelings which go back to the original separation between mother and child. Donald Winnicott calls this "phenomenal death" and states: "What happened in the past was death as a phenomenon, but not as the sort of fact that we observe. Many men and women spend their lives wondering whether to find a solution by suicide, that is, sending the body to death which has already happened to the psyche." In other words, suicide is an attempt, on the part of the person in pain, to concretize or actualize something which is felt to have already happened, but which they can't remember experiencing.

Winnicott goes on to say, "Suicide is not the answer, however, but is a despair gesture." In the case of adoptees, there is a re-experiencing of the mother's not being there when she should have been bonding with him. The feeling of despair is a response to a sense of nothing happening when it should be happening. Winnicott claims, "It is easier for a patient to remember trauma than to remember nothing happening, when it might have happened." Many suicidal people, although they can think of nothing in their present lives to make them feel so desperate as to commit suicide, nevertheless are sure that suicide is the only answer to their feelings of despair. Winnicott feels that a simple acknowledgment that the person "died" in infancy (which for the infant has the meaning of annihilation) can prevent the actual suicide attempt.

I believe that birthmothers, many of whom have been hospitalized for attempted suicide, experience similar feelings of desperation. They are physiologically, emotionally, and spiritually ready to welcome into the world and bond with their babies, but never have the chance to do so. They, too, are left with the feeling of waiting for something to happen that never happens. They experience the black hole of despair, instead of the pure, white light of union with the child.

It is important for those who feel suicidal to realize that they lived through feelings of despair when the sense of longing for something to happen actually took place and they can live through them again. In the present, those feelings are *only* feelings, and feelings can't kill. Although tremendously painful, feelings can be tolerated. If a person becomes so inundated by the feelings that he is out of touch with the adult, intellectual side of himself, tragedy can happen.

Loss and the Mourning Process

Even if there is a loss or some other crisis currently going on in the life of the adoptee which convinces him that there is a legitimate reason for wanting to end his life, this present loss is probably also triggering the feelings of the first loss, thus exacerbating the pain and making it *seem* intolerable. As an adult, he must engage the intellectual aspect of himself when choosing whether to act or not act on those archaic, baby feelings. These suicidal feelings, a feeling perhaps for the adoptee that he really doesn't exist and for the birthmother that she doesn't have the right to exist, are the result of past experiences and should never be acted upon in the present.

Summary

A sense of loss expressed by most adoptees often seems to manifest in sadness and depression. This might be interpreted as an unconscious yearning for the lost love object (the first mother?) or in a feeling of incompleteness (the lost part of the Self?). The age at which a child is relinquished might have something to do with which of the two predominates. In any case, the result appears to be a loss of a sense of goodness of self and mistrust of the permanency of future relationships with significant others.

The stages of grief through which an abandoned child will pass include rage and protestation, a sense of hopelessness and despair, detachment, and finally a kind of resignation and the beginning of attachment to the substitute mother. If an adoptive mother, being especially tuned in to her baby, experiences his hesitation in attaching, she may feel it as rejection. She should, instead, understand this as the child's need to protect *himself* from rejection.

The unconscious fear of further losses, which threatens annihilation, causes anxiety. This anxiety may manifest in behavior designed to make the parents understand the chaos the child is feeling inside (acting out) or in withdrawal and psychosomatic symptoms. Both responses are protecting the child from a more severe state of psychological deterioration. A more dangerous response to a sense of impending doom is that of suicidal ideation. In children suicidal thoughts get acted out in risky behavior (such as engaging in dangerous activities, driving recklessly, taking drugs, etc.), whereas most adults are more overt in attempting to end their despair.

Many adoptees say that they tolerate death better than they tolerate separations. They may respond to loss by denying it, becoming numb to it, or by trying to avoid it. Trying to avoid loss causes many adoptees to avoid intimate relationships. This is just one of the many consequences of the devastating loss suffered at or near the beginning of their lives. Those and other manifestations of the primal wound will be discussed next.

PART TWO

The Manifestations

(The pain of adoption) is something that can lie dormant most of one's life. If it erupts in childhood, adolescence, or early adulthood and is dismissed as neurotic behavior or normal rebellion, it can subside into numbness. But it can stir malignantly in some adoptees all their lives, making them detached, floating, unable to love or to trust. . . . (Adoption) has got to be understood.

    —BETTY JEAN LIFTON

With this statement adoptee, author, and friend B. J. Lifton has eloquently expressed what many adoptees have felt for a long time; yet adoption is still proclaimed by many people in our society as a simple and ideal solution to what is actually an extremely complex and painful problem. In the first part of this book, I presented my premise that the separation from the birthmother causes a primal or narcissistic wound to the Self of the adopted child. How, then, does this wound manifest in the lives of this population?

Perhaps the most easily observed manifestation is difficulties in relationships. This is certainly one of the most prevalent presenting problems for adoptees in counseling. When one gets beneath the surface of the relationship problem, one can find some common themes: symptoms of depression and anxiety which reflect a sense of loss and basic mistrust and which in turn result in emotional problems. All of these symptoms interfere with healthy relationships, and all can be traced back to the primal wound and the many ways in which it may have been exacerbated in the adoptive relationship by parents unaware of the original trauma.

In this part of the book, then, I will try to convey the ways in which the adopted population seems to be affected by the early trauma of separation from the birthmother. In doing so, I will be reporting my experience of adoption from both my personal and professional perspectives, including my research and my clinical work with adoptees, birthmothers, and adoptive families.

One of the difficulties in doing research in adoption is that members of the adoption triad frequently use denial and avoidance as defenses against painful feelings. These defenses must be understood as unconscious on the part of the person who is using them. It is not as if one decides to deny or avoid something. Although one can certainly do that, when we speak of denial and avoidance as *defense mechanisms*, we are speaking of something which happens automatically in the unconscious: the blocking out of painful experiences in order to cope with one's situation. This is why it is so difficult to get through or overcome these defenses: One is totally unaware that one is employing them!

There are forms of denial and avoidance which are more conscious, however. One example is the wish on the part of adoptive parents that adopting children is no different from giving birth to them. It is my belief that this wish, which is a willful denial of reality, brings into play many reactions, responses, and behaviors on the part of the adoptive parents which are detrimental to the healthy development of their children.

The Manifestations

The taboo against talking about adoption as being different from a "natural" family is very strong, not only within the families themselves, but in society as a whole. For instance, there were people who, when hearing about my research, wondered why I wanted to "rock the boat" or "upset the status quo" by introducing such controversial ideas as infants being able to differentiate between their birthmothers and their adoptive mothers. I find it revealing that *none of those who objected was an adoptee.*

I believe that where there is reluctance to openly discuss an issue, there is something which needs to be clarified and understood. To those who asked me, when they heard of my study, "Why would the separation from the birthmother affect a newborn baby?", I had to admit that I, at one time, asked the same question myself. Now, however, I believe the more appropriate question to be, "How could the separation from the mother to whom he was connected for nine months *not* affect an infant?" In the theoretical part of this book I have suggested that the separation does affect the child drastically, even if the effects are not easy to detect because of the child's coping mechanisms.

With one or two exceptions, neither the participants of my original research nor the adult adoptees in my practice have been identified as needing treatment as children. For the most part they represent adoptees who were acquiescent and compliant as children, rather than "testing out." As adults most of them lead ordinary lives and do not stand out as having significant problems. Nevertheless, they felt as if adoption were something that they wanted to talk about, although many could not say why. Perhaps we can get a clue, again from Lifton, who began her book *Twice Born* this way:

> I am adopted. You wouldn't know it to meet me. To all outward appearances I am a writer, a married woman, a mother, a theater buff, an animal fanatic—yes, I can pass. But locked within me there is an adopted child who stirs guilty and ambivalent even as I write these words. The adopted child can never grow up. Who has ever heard of an adopted adult?

51

Perhaps the urge to talk about their adoption has been an attempt on the part of many adoptees to begin to understand the adopted child within them so that as adults they might learn to know themselves more completely and thereby become more complete.

CHAPTER 5

Love, Trust, and the Adoptive Mother

The child who is placed with adoptive parents at or soon after birth misses the mutual and deeply satisfying mother-child relationship, the roots of which lie in that deep area of the personality where the physiological and the psychological are merged. Both for the child and for the natural mother, that period is part of a biological sequence, and it is to be doubted whether the relationship of the child to its post-partum mother, in its subtler effects, can be replaced by even the best of substitute mothers.

    —FLORENCE CLOTHIER

The Limitations of the Adoptive Mother

Clothier made this observation fifty years ago! Was hers a voice lost in the wilderness? It was twenty-five to thirty years later that other professionals, such as Donald Winnicott and Joseph Chilton Pearce, began to say the same thing: There is something special which happens to prepare a mother for the birth of her baby, a sequence of events which begins at conception and which cannot be learned or acquired "by even the best of substitute mothers."

The adoptive parents, who have been waiting for a baby and who feel ready to love and nurture him, come into the picture at a disadvantage. In fact there are four areas of concern about which they may not have been made aware: (1) The mother has not had the benefit of the forty-week preparation period of gestation, (2) neither parent may have been alerted to the fact that their baby has suffered a trauma upon having been separated from his biological mother, (3) most adoptive parents have not dealt with their feelings about their own losses, including the loss of fertility, and (4) those who already have biological children may not have adequately explored their reasons for wanting to adopt or the impact this will have on their family life.

Despite these deficiencies, the mother usually attaches very quickly to the baby and loves him as her own. Most of the time, because she has had no previous experience with which to compare what she is now experiencing, she notices nothing unusual. And even if she is very perceptive and does notice some difficulty in the bonding process between her and her new baby, she may have no clear understanding of it, because she has not had adequate preparation for it. She has not been told that the baby is mourning for his first mother.

If the adoptive mother has a child who acts out his pain, she may begin to notice it by the age of eighteen months to three years and wonder if she is doing something wrong. The lack of information about the original trauma may make her feel inadequate and somehow at fault. If she has a compliant child, she may not notice anything at all (until adolescence, when the task of defining one's identity may bring with it a change in the behavior of the child).

In any case, the relationship with the mother, whether conflicted or compliant, is the most crucial and the most ambivalent relationship for the child. She is the person to whom he wants most to connect and the person with whom it seems the most dangerous. A mother can't be trusted: She may be an abandoner.

Who Is the Abandoner?

Herbert Wieder claims that often the confusion about the meaning of adoption as a process is reflected in the child's confusion about which mother is which: The child confuses the adopting mother with the abandoning mother and mistakes the term adoption for abandonment. Here again the problem is seen as an intellectual dilemma rather than as inner confusion. While I agree with Wieder that the *concept* of adoption may be confusing for the child, I believe that it is his actual *experience* of the abandonment which causes him to project the abandoning mother upon the adoptive mother: She is, after all, available, while the birthmother is not.

The child's perception of the adoptive mother vacillates between his seeing her as the rescuing mother and as the abandoning mother. As a result the child demonstrates ambivalent feelings of compliance and hostility in his attitude toward her. These feelings, which are protecting the child against vulnerability and possible annihilation, are confusing to both mother and child.

This confusion is further noticed as adoptees alternately refer to their biological mothers and their adoptive mothers as the "real" mother. My observation has been that the term "real" is used consciously for the adoptive mother: "My real parents are the parents who raised me." Yet, as adoptees become more relaxed, when they say "real mother," they mean the biological mother: "I love my adoptive parents, but I need to find my real mother."

Even if the child recognizes that the adoptive mother is not the abandoning mother, she certainly *could* become one. After all, if it happened once, it could happen again. Frederick Stone points out that the question, whether spoken or unspoken, "Why did my own mother not keep me?" is almost always followed by the unexpressed but equally anxious thought, "If she could do that, what about you?"

Splitting

The question "Who was the abandoner?" and the subsequent projection onto the adoptive mother the role of the abandoner is often experienced as a phenomenon called "splitting," in which a child assigns all "good" attributes to one set of parents and all "bad" attributes to the other. Even a child who does not have more than one set of parents, will, when feeling rejected by a parent, fantasize that he is not really the child of this rejecting parent, but that he will be rescued by another all-loving parent who will let him do what he wants. Freud called this the "family romance" theory.

This fantasy takes on more reality for children who actually do have two sets of parents. Instead of seeing both aspects of good and bad in one set of parents, an adoptee often assigns one attribute to the adoptive parents and the other to the biological parents. Sometimes the good image is given to the adoptive mother and the negative aspect is for the biological mother who gave him away. Frequently, however, using the mechanisms of reversal and displacement (in which one's feelings for a particular person are projected onto another more convenient person—like yelling at one's wife, when one is really mad at one's boss), the adoptee projects the negative image onto the adoptive mother in an effort to work out feelings of hostility, anger, and rejection as a result of having been relinquished. Because the adoptive mother doesn't understand what is going on, she often reacts negatively to this behavior, thus giving the child a "real" reason to be angry at her.

It has been shown that regardless of the intellectual reasons a child has been given for his relinquishment, there are often feelings of betrayal, anger, resentment, and sadness, which are projected onto the available mother-figure. It is equally true that babies who have been "abandoned" to incubators, or who have been separated as the result of some catastrophe such as war, will need to work out the anger and lack of trust which result. The difference is that in the latter two cases, the person with whom he or she tries to work it out is the biological mother herself, not a substitute for her.

If the adoptive mother is insecure about her own sense of being the child's mother (and I believe that in a certain sense there is good reason for this feeling of insecurity), a child can exert a great deal of power over her by using this split to his advantage. The "mean" adoptive mother is not, after all, the "real" mother, and the child doesn't have to pay attention to her. The adoptive mother may give in and allow the child to misbehave in order to regain his love. Or, feeling rejected herself, she may act in an angry, rejecting manner towards him, thus setting up a vicious cycle of anger, rejection, anxiety, and capitulation, resulting in a confusion of inconsistency in parenting, and acting-out by the child.

This scenario is sometimes played out in reverse, where the child, having been told that he is "special," feels that he has to be perfect in order to retain the love and acceptance of his parents. This need to be special can put a great deal of pressure on the child to live up to some perceived expectations which are frequently unattainable. This often leaves the child feeling inadequate and worthless, a reinforcement of his feelings of having failed his first mother. The need to be perfect for the "rescuing" parents makes the child suppress his own true self in order to submit to the wishes of his parents. This seems imperative to his survival. As Wieder notes: "You have to be good or you're gotten rid of."

On Being Special

The feeling of needing to be perfect, but feeling imperfect, becomes even more confusing in reference to the story that many adoptees are told, which is that they are chosen. What does this mean to them? Some say that being chosen means being special; but what does "special" mean? Among those I interviewed, only one interpreted this as meaning that her parents chose her and everyone else had to take what they got, which is how many parents believe all adoptees interpret it. This is not the popular interpretation, however. In answering the question Irene said, "Not a damn thing, because *I* had no choice!" Betty said that "chosen" to her meant that her parents had chosen to have a child, but not necessarily her. Teresa said that when she got older, she realized that it was her parents who were chosen (by the agency), not she.

Being told that they are chosen or special seems to be confusing and to put a great deal of pressure on many adoptees to live up to a variety of perceived expectations on the part of their parents. One of those expectations means behaving in such a way as to ensure that their parents do not feel hurt or threatened by their questions, actions, or attitudes. Janice told me that she felt that she had to be the perfect child, so that her parents could be the perfect parents.

Taichert and Harvin, in speaking to the issue of a child's feeling unable to fulfill his parents' altruistic or other emotional needs, mentions the message which many children get about feeling grateful toward their parents: "Put in this position, the child is prevented from expressing his feelings, differences of opinion, or even his creative ideas. He can neither gripe nor complain, lest he appear ungrateful for his good fortune."

Many of the adoptees with whom I talked felt grateful that their adoptive parents were providing them with a home and family. Some adoptees responded to this gratitude by trying to prove that they were worthy of this kindness. They are the high achievers among the adoptive population, who feel the need to get one more degree, to strive for more and more approval, not only from their parents but also from society—as if to justify their existence. Internally, however, high achiever or not, the burden of this obligation to be dutiful and thankful for his adoption may either make a child cautious and unable to express his needs or feelings, or it may make him seem indifferent and callous. In any case, it may cause him to view his differentness as undesirable and something about which to be ashamed.

Denise voiced what many feel: "Being chosen by your adoptive parents doesn't mean anything compared to being unchosen by your birthmother." This feeling of being "unchosen" sets the adoptee up for many roadblocks to normal emotional development.

Images of Love and Hate

One area of development where there is a noticeable difficulty is in the task of integrating the feelings of love and hate into one person. The splitting of the images of good and bad between the birth and adoptive parents, as mentioned earlier, often impedes the ability of the adopted child to accept his adoptive parents as having both a good and a bad side with which he must work out his feelings of love and hate. It also hinders his working out these feelings toward himself. Adoptees tend to split the images of good and bad, not only for their parents, but for themselves as well. Many adoptees have told me that they see themselves as having an innate "badness" or flaw, which got them kicked out of paradise in the first place and which threatens to trigger another rejection. They see themselves as unloved and unlovable. Even if this is not conscious, it will be evident in their relationships with others.

The need to be good often causes adopted children to be hypervigilant, which means that they are constantly assessing the "climate" of the environment in order to know how to behave. They feel as if their security within the family requires it. This need to be vigilant in trying to determine what is expected of them feels like walking a tightrope or walking on eggshells to many adoptees. Or, as Joan puts it, "It's like walking a narrow ridge in the middle of the Grand Canyon."

The anxiety which this provokes sometimes leads to exaggerated behavior. Allison, who never caused problems for her parents and who says that she always felt loved in her family, nevertheless describes her relationship with her mother as "love-hate." She says, "My anger at my mother was way out of proportion to what was going on. I would just explode." She would sometimes get fevers when she would "flip out." She doesn't remember her mother ever getting mad at her or raising her voice, but she felt manipulated by her and angry at her. The feeling of being manipulated (about which I will have more to say later) makes sense in view of an adoptee's early experience, but may not have much to do with what is going on in the present and interferes with the building of trust.

A Matter of Trust

In his work on the Life Cycle, Erik Erikson tells us that the first crucial stage for healthy human development is *Trust vs. Mistrust.* One of the ways a baby learns to trust in his own sense of goodness and in his mother to be there for him is the sense of security he derives from her meeting his needs, both physical and emotional. Here again, the adoptive mother is at a disadvantage, because the infant has already experienced the mother as not having been there. The environment is hostile, the mother can go away, love can be withdrawn, and aspects of the Self can be lost. She therefore cannot be trusted.

This lack of trust is demonstrated over and over again in adoptees' relationships throughout their lives. There is always the expectation, beginning with the adoptive mother, that the loved one will go away. Caroline puts it this way: "Intellectually I knew that my mother would not leave me. After all, she never gave me any reason to doubt her. But in my heart I didn't believe it. She *could* leave . . . if I didn't toe the line. It's the same with my women friends. I'm constantly surprised that they remember me. I think that if they're not with me, they'll forget me."

Love is Dangerous!

This inability to trust the permanence of the mother/child relationship may also be at the root of many adoptees' failure to feel love and affection from the adoptive mother. No matter how much or how often a child is shown or told that he is loved, he is unable to believe it. One adoptive mother said, "Over and over again I show Ann how much I love her, how precious she is to me, but I always feel as if she doesn't believe me. There is some kind of barrier there that I can't penetrate."

Love, Trust, and the Adoptive Mother

Jennifer, who didn't feel loved by her mother, said, "My mother took good care of me and gave me every material advantage, but she never hugged and kissed me. I learned a lot from her, but so far as being a loving, demonstrative person, she wasn't." While it may be true that this was not a demonstrative mother, it might also be true, as was once the case between my daughter and me, that the adoptee was not able to allow her mother to be affectionate, but needed instead to keep a distance as a way to be less vulnerable. Although the distancing may seem to be coming from the adoptive mother, through a process called "projective identification," it may actually be coming from the adoptee as a defense against vulnerability.

My experience with my daughter is a case in point: I wanted to hold and cuddle my daughter, but she seemed uncomfortable whenever I did so. As a baby she wanted to be in a vertical position most of the time and wiggled around whenever I tried to rock her in the rocking chair or to hug and kiss her. I once mentioned this to an adoptee named Geri and noted that it was different when we were in public. There my daughter became very affectionate herself and allowed for more closeness from me. I said that I attributed this to her feeling that we couldn't get too close in public. But Geri said, "Oh, no! I know what she was doing. She knew you wouldn't dare reject her in public, so she could allow her true feelings and needs to surface." One learns from those who know!

If a child, even an infant, doesn't trust the love and permanency of the relationship, why should he put himself in a position to be hurt again? Is it not possible that in many cases the adoptee will feel the need to defend against a further devastation by initiating a distancing response to bonding? This seems to ring true for those adoptees who, either through regression or hypnosis, have felt the need to "take care of themselves" or to guard against vulnerability by rejecting love.

This distancing may be there even when the child seems compliant and affectionate. Many adoptees have noted an inability to feel truly intimate with their adoptive mothers. Even when describing the

61

relationship with the mother as positive, this is often qualified by statements that the relationship has been shallow or superficial. Donna, who felt quite connected to her mother and modeled herself after her, says that she now realizes that the relationship was shallow emotionally: "I cannot discuss intimate feelings with her." She described herself as "numbing out" her own feelings and aligning herself with her mother, becoming what her mother wanted "a la Alice Miller." (Author's note: The adoptee was referring to a book by Alice Miller *The Drama of the Gifted Child*.)

Vivian, who began by saying that she and her adoptive mother get along fine, also said that it is difficult for them to talk very deeply about things and that they always end up arguing. This was also my experience with my daughter, unless it was late at night when her defenses were down, or when we were talking on the telephone. The distance provided by the telephone gave her the security she needed to say what was in her heart. She could allow intimacy in conversation so long as she didn't feel threatened by my presence.

Bill blames his lack of communication with his mother on himself. Describing the relationship between him and his adoptive mother as open and positive, he nevertheless says that he doesn't talk with her very much. "I'm not a very talkative person." Many times the distancing, coldness, or lack of affection is *projected* upon the adoptive mother as a defensive attitude and then *felt* as coming from her.

Evelyn, who didn't equivocate about her positive relationship with her adoptive mother, describing many positive memories of mother/ daughter activities, has very strong and angry feelings toward her birthmother. Her adoptive mother is obviously the "good" mother.

The Relationship with the Father

The ambivalent and often conflictual relationship which ensues with the mother is sometimes in contrast to that with the adoptive father. This relationship, while not always positive, seems fairly consistent. Some adoptees find it easier to connect with their fathers than with their mothers. Frequently, however, fathers are either absent or emotionally distant, placing most of the responsibility for the child's emotional well-being on the mother. For those whose fathers are not distant, the relationship seems more straightforward and easier to define than that with the mother. Fathers are often confused by the conflict between the child and the mother, because he is not directly affected by it. There is an intense, ambivalent energy which happens between mother and child, which the father neither understands nor supports. Melanie puts it this way: "It was between me and Mom. Dad was outside it." The father does not understand that the child is trying to connect with the mother, while at the same time is terrified to do so. The vulnerability which a trusting, loving relationship with her might present is what makes the mother/child relationship so ambivalent and difficult.

The Withdrawal/Acting Out Dichotomy

The anxiety generated by the uncertainty of the permanence of the caregiver results in feelings toward her which are ambivalent, conflictual, and vacillating. These feelings appear to cause the child to assume one of two diametrically opposed attitudes toward her: aggressive, provocative, and anti-social, or withdrawn, acquiescent, and compliant. When there are two adopted children in a family, in every case that I have studied, one adoptee assumes the acting-out role and the other is compliant, regardless of their birth order, sex, or personalities. In most cases in the literature, due to these being adoptees in treatment, the hostility was overt and the compliance was covert. For most of the adoptees I interviewed, however, it has been the other way around: They act in their families in an acquiescent, compliant manner.

The anger and hostility are there, however, and burst forth unexpectedly at times. Andrew describes it this way: "I would be withdrawn and quiet, then all of a sudden do something 'off the wall,'" which everyone would consider his not being himself. The problem is that, as with many adoptees, the "not-being-himself" part is the way he actually feels a great deal of the time, but can't express for fear of rejection. Francie refers to her withdrawal as "hiding out." The "hiding out," "numbing out," or living the "false self" may seem a matter of survival.

Roberta, another adoptee who acted compliant as a child, says that at about third grade she became very angry. "Something darkened —there was a psychological and emotional shift." These feelings seemed dangerous and needed to be kept hidden. After having been in therapy for five years, Roberta mentioned to her therapist that she was adopted. He dismissed this as unimportant since she had a "good" adoptive family! This attitude is what makes many adoptees and adoptive families frustrated with clinicians.

The Nurturing Mother

Despite the limitations placed upon the adoptive mother, she can and does make a big difference in the life of her child. Although she cannot erase the scars left by the original separation, she is the nurturing mother, the mother who feeds him, rocks him, kisses his skinned knees, helps him with his homework, and goes with him to select a gift for his girlfriend. She does that which the birthmother cannot do, and, in most cases, she does it well.

Some adoptees have told me, after being reunited with their birthmothers, that despite the pain of having been relinquished and growing up in a family of people unrelated to them, they have felt that they were given better opportunities than otherwise would have been available to them. One has to keep in mind that this is an intellectual assessment and has to be balanced against the immense psychic pain of the original separation.

The Right to Selfhood

Part of this pain has to do with the adoptee's not being allowed (or his perception of not being allowed) to be himself. As Steven

Nickman points out, it is reasonable to believe that an adoptee will be different from his adoptive parents. Because of his need for self-definition and his inability to identify with either of his adoptive parents, an adoptee may be even more prone than other children to rebel against parental expectations, which may be completely at odds with that which he perceives to be true about himself. The problem of not being allowed to be oneself can also exist in biological families, but in adoptive families, where there are separate origins, the problem is magnified. Many times the only way in which a child can feel secure in his environment is to do what is expected of him and inhibit his true sense of Self.

This attitude of conformity and compliance was voiced by many of the adoptees whom I interviewed. Victoria said that she knew that she would not please her parents unless she became an attorney, which she tried to do, but this felt like the farthest thing from her core being. "I felt that I was acting out my father's wish for himself and that he had no idea who I was or what I might want for myself."

Jim, who rebelled against his father's wishes, said, "I would sit for hours at the piano, knowing that my father would rather have had me out playing baseball. But that wasn't me. I just couldn't do it, even though I knew that I was disappointing him."

Sometimes there is a sense of responsibility toward the unborn natural child of the adoptive parents. Dorothy says that she always tried, but never quite "lived up to my mother's expectations of what her own daughter would have been like." The burden of trying to live up to some perceived expectations, whether real or imagined, may exacerbate the ambivalent feelings many adoptees already have toward their adoptive families and toward their adopted status in general. In my conversations with adoptees and their parents, it is clear that sometimes the adoptees' perceptions are correct, and sometimes they are more a reflection of their own feelings of inadequacy, which they are projecting upon their parents.

Summary

Because there is reason to believe that during gestation a mother becomes uniquely sensitized to her baby, it is to be questioned whether it is possible for the adoptive mother, lacking this special preparation, to bond with the baby in the same way as his biological mother might have done. In addition to this, the child's experience of abandonment causes him to mistrust the permanence of the present caretaker and to defend against further loss by distancing himself from her. This often causes the adoptive mother to feel rejected and to act in an angry, rejecting manner towards her child, setting up a cycle of rejection and inconsistent treatment and behavior.

The question of who is the real abandoner is sometimes confusing for the child, since most often he has no conscious memory of the birthmother. The role of abandoner often gets projected onto the adoptive mother as the child tries to express his rage at having been abandoned. In doing so he often splits the images of "good" and "bad" parent between the two sets of parents. He seeks to protect himself from further rejection by distancing himself from intimacy with the adoptive mother. Despite his ambivalence toward her, an adoptive mother can make a big difference in her child's life by giving him love, care, and nurturing which his biological mother is not able to do. Since in most cases the child had no connection to the birthfather, the adoptive father, at least as a symbol, is not seen as dangerous, and the relationship with him is less conflicted and ambivalent than that with the mother.

Anxiety, which is produced by the uncertainty of the permanence of the mother-figure, is sometimes expressed in disguised form and often manifests itself in two diametric behavior patterns: provocative, aggressive, and impulsive; or withdrawn, compliant, and acquiescent. Where there are two adopted children in a family, they appear to assume a polarity in their overt behavioral patterns, no matter what their personalities are like. Both are wounded, but each is responding to the pain and anxiety in a different way. Each has the same wish for love and acceptance, and each has the same fears of rejection and abandonment. One pushes for the inevitable and the other guards against it. In neither case is the child operating from his true Self, but from a false self, which helps protect him from further hurt, rejection, and disappointment.

It is very difficult for the adoptive mother of a newborn baby to take in the concept of the primal wound. It is abhorrent; it is heartbreaking; it is something she would rather not think about. And many adoptive mothers don't think about it. The mother sees what looks like a normal baby, a baby who in many ways *is* normal, and later sees a laughing, happy toddler, and she can't believe that this child is aching inside. But if she is really alert, if she is truly attuned to her child, she will notice the sadness, the pain, the fear. And in so noticing, she will be better able to help him to allow her to love him, and for him to love her in return.

CHAPTER 6

The Core Issues: Abandonment and Loss

One of the most common fears is that of being abandoned. Abandonment is a dominant theme in child myths.

—HARRIET MACHTIGER

Loss of a loved person is one of the most intensely painful experiences any human being can suffer. And not only is it painful to experience but it is also painful to witness, if only because we are so impotent to help. To the bereaved nothing but the return of the lost person can bring true comfort; should what we provide fall short of that it is felt almost as an insult. . . . There is a tendency to underestimate how intensely distressing and disabling loss usually is and for how long the distress, and often the disablement, commonly lasts. Conversely, there is a tendency to suppose that a normal healthy person can and should get over a bereavement not only fairly rapidly but also completely.

—JOHN BOWLBY

The Profoundness of Loss

If the primal experience for the adopted child is abandonment, then the core issues are loss and the fear of a further abandonment. Neither is acknowledged in most adoptive families, since the abandonment occurred so early in the child's life. Given no acknowledgment of his loss or tools to help him grieve, the child copes in whatever way he can, ways which manifest in behavior that is often misunderstood.

Loss itself is not very well understood in our society. We tend to deny its importance on many levels. We get married and celebrate the joy of the new phase of life without ever considering that there may be a loss involved, much less that we might need to mourn that loss. Or a couple has a baby and sends out the happy announcements, while neither dares think about the loss of a different kind of relationship, what impact a new family member will have on them, and that grieving might be in order. There is no permission in our society to recognize in each of life's transitions the polarities between gain and loss or joy and sorrow. We are expected to be happy, sing songs, dance jigs, but never to mourn.

Just as we have few rituals or rites of passage in our society to help us through transition periods, neither do we value the more negative aspects of those periods. We are a society in which we want everything to be "nice" or positive, and one in which we try to ignore or get through as soon as possible everything that is painful or difficult. We have a great deal of difficulty accepting, understanding, or even acknowledging that it may be paradox and polarity that give life energy and excitement, the impetus toward movement, the aspiration toward change and growth.

If we do recognize that someone has suffered a loss, one that we *cannot* ignore such as the death of a parent, spouse, or child, we can only tolerate the bereaved person's grief for so long and then we expect him or her to "get on with life." As Bowlby puts it, " . . . there is a tendency to suppose that a normal healthy person can and should

69

get over a bereavement not only fairly rapidly but also completely."
So, with little permission to fully acknowledge or mourn our losses,
we deny them; we send them down into the depths of the unconscious,
where they rule our lives in many insidious ways, causing feelings and
behavior which are then sometimes labeled as pathological.

The Pathologizing of Abandonment and Loss

Yet is it possible to completely recover from a devastating loss,
such as a child's loss of his mother or a mother's loss of her child?
What is meant by a pathological response to loss? We seem to be a
nation of depressed people. Are we all, in some sense, pathological?
Depression may be a sign of unresolved grief. If we gave permission
and had the rituals for grieving our myriad and varied losses in life,
would we then be a more healthy people, a happier people? Would
we then be able to function better in our society?

And what about anxiety? Perhaps the anxiety felt by so many
people signals a greater incidence of childhood trauma than we would
like to admit. In addition to the now recognized trauma of child
physical, sexual, and emotional abuse, I propose to add the trauma
of the separation of a child from its mother. It is difficult to change
our thinking about adoption from that of a wonderful, altruistic event
to that of a traumatic, terrifying experience for the child. It is difficult,
and understandably so, for the adoptive parents to look at the infant
and think that he might be suffering. Yet how can he not be? Except
in the case of some truly enlightened adoptive mothers, there is no
acknowledgment of the child's loss of the original mother. Therefore,
there is no permission, either implicit or explicit, to mourn.

As the adoptee matures, the grief goes on, unresolved. Depression
and anxiety persist, yet because most adopted children are placed with
their adoptive parents as infants, clinicians fail to consider trauma and
unresolved grief as the causes of their anxiety and depression, thereby
missing an opportunity for effective treatment.

The Core Issues: Abandonment and Loss

There is no doubt that the grieving person needs help. When one has suffered a loss at the beginning of life, before conscious memory, there is a need to work through this loss in order for the person to function well later in life, both personally and professionally. If we think of unresolved grief as pathological, we should do so only in the sense that it hinders efficiency. The adoptee's emotional reactions to past events are normal and need to be validated. At the same time they must be seen as maladaptive in the present and a hindrance to full functioning. Precious energy gets diverted in many ways: First is the need to stave off another rejection and loss. Later, as the child begins to sense on a more conscious level that he is different from those who are nurturing him, energy is diverted to the tremendous effort it takes to "fit in" with the adoptive family. Or there may be an even more basic need to prove that he has a right to exist in the world.

Depression as a result of unresolved grief, and anxiety caused by a long-forgotten trauma and a concomitant sense of impending doom (another abandonment) work in tandem and often restrict the full functioning of an adoptee's emotional and intellectual capacities. George described it "like trying to walk under water; there is so much resistance. If I could rid myself of anxiety, everything would be so easy." Other adoptees talk about an underlying sadness which seems constant and pervasive, a hindrance to real joy. Ana Maria puts it this way, "Even when I'm having fun, there is a shadow inside me, something which keeps me from ever experiencing joy or what I think joy might be."

Post-Traumatic Stress Disorder

If depression and anxiety are twin symptoms for adoptees, the closest diagnosis might best be described as post-traumatic stress disorder. Because the early source of symptoms is often overlooked, however, this diagnosis is not recognized. An adoptee may demonstrate the tell-tale signs of anxiety or fear, helplessness, loss of control, and threat of annihilation; yet, unless there is evidence of child abuse, he is not seen as having suffered trauma.

There are other signs of trauma: intrusion, a traumatic memory of that first abandonment, and constriction, a shutting down or surrendering to the situation at hand (being in the "wrong" family). I was referring to intrusion when I talked about suicidal ideation for the adoptee and the meaning this might have. Intrusion makes him alert to a possible repetition of a past trauma or the feeling that one needs to facilitate it (the threat of annihilation or the urge to make concrete an experience he thought he might have had, but can't remember—dying). Even if the present environment is safe, it may not feel that way. Traumatic memories, in the form of emotional or bodily sensations, keep intruding into consciousness. This often causes the adoptee to appear irritable, aggressive, impulsive, and anti-social.

In the case of constriction or numbing, the adoptee is in another state of consciousness, where he can't be hurt by painful memories. This state is characterized by emotional detachment, indifference, complacency, and passivity. This is the state adoptees are in when everyone thinks he is daydreaming. It is almost as if he is in trance. Teachers complain about this state in school children. Schoolwork is difficult, because it often involves memory—something the adoptee is trying to keep at bay.

Adoptees vacillate between intrusion and constriction, with one or the other being his normal way of operating in the world, and the other insinuating itself into his behavior from time to time. This leaves him feeling paralyzed, unable to integrate the trauma and to get on with life. There is also an existential dilemma, whereby he is unable to make sense of either natural or divine order: Mothers are not supposed to leave their babies. God should not let it happen. No rationalization changes that basic *knowing*.

Like other victims of trauma, adoptees often turn their rage at the unspeakable thing that happened to them on their caretakers. Although some reunited adoptees speak of feeling rage for their birth-mothers or for the society which caused their separation from her, many will say that they feel no ill-will toward her, but have all their lives exhibited oppositional behavior and intense rage toward their adoptive parents. Paradoxically they feel a tremendous dependency upon and need to connect to those same adoptive parents. This ambivalence is the source of great confusion and enigmatic behavior.

Not understanding the unconscious source of this behavior, parents think that their children should be able to change it at will. There is often a feeling that if the child would just "shape up," just try harder, he would be able to do better (in relating to them, in making and keeping the right kinds of friends, in his school work, etc.). Yet, in talking to adult adoptees who acted out as children or adolescents, they, of course, don't understand it any more than their parents do. Michael told me, "I put my parents through hell, and I don't know why. They were good parents. They did their best and always stuck by me. But I was always mad at them, feeling manipulated by them, and striking out at them. I couldn't seem to help it. It was coming from a dark part of me that I had no control over. I feel terrible about it, and yet I am still not able to have a loving relationship with them, and I just don't know why." The idea that he was reacting to a trauma that he didn't even remember had never occurred to him. He just thought he was a bad kid.

When treatment is sought, it is usually only for the "bad kid," the acting-out child. The "good kid," as constricted and shut down as he may be, is not seen as having any problems. One reason that the difficult child is sent into treatment is that the parents can no longer cope with his behavior. And with good reason: The provocation and aggression caused by the anxiety about a further rejection become more and more destructive and unbearable to the parents as the child tests their commitment to him. The provocative behavior often plays into the parents' insecurities about being good enough parents and into their own rejection issues. They then become defensive and retaliatory, instead of understanding and steadfast. Sadly, their defensive reactions often produce the very outcome which the adoptee feared in the first place: abandonment—being sent out of the home to residential treatment centers, boarding schools, or simply out on the street. If the adoptees' behaviors were seen as attempts to avoid pain, rather than deliberate provocation of the parents, the parents might be able to identify the signs or manifestations of that trauma and help their child integrate it.

The Manifestations of Separation and Loss in Childhood

What are the ways in which one can detect the wounds of abandonment and loss in children? In addition to those criteria already mentioned (the stages of grief through which an infant passes, somatic responses to loss, separation anxiety upon entering day care or school or going away to camp, the sabotaging of birthday parties and other anniversary reactions, and the loss of the Self), there are some other responses which I want to mention or some upon which I would like to expand. One of these is the numbing of affect or feelings.

The Numbing of Affect

One of the ways in which parents can detect a problem with loss in a compliant child is the way in which he responds to death or separation. What happens when a pet dies? How does he react when a grandparent is buried? What is his reaction to overnight separations or visits to relatives without the parents? When our two daughters would visit their grandparents for a few days, it was my older, adopted daughter who would call after the first day and say that she thought she'd better come back home. This always surprised me, not only because she loved her grandparents, but because she seemed to have such a difficult time relating to me. I thought she'd relish a break from our confrontations. What I didn't understand was that the anxiety which produced both the oppositional behavior and the fear of being away from me had the same root cause: the fear of abandonment.

The Core Issues: Abandonment and Loss

Loss can cause a complete change in behavioral patterns. Bella, who was quite close to her father, didn't mourn him very much when he died, although she was only 13 years old at the time. She has always wondered about this. What did happen was that she suffered a dramatic behavioral change, going from provocative and aggressive to quiet, withdrawn, and compliant. She "decided" to be good and perfect at everything. Her grades improved dramatically. She became totally withdrawn, because "being otherwise wasn't worth the risk anymore." She wasn't sure what the risk was, but it is possible that it was the loss of another parent (about which she would feel responsible). Despite losses, she managed to keep functioning by conscious effort. When she began to feel too much, she cut off her feelings. She allowed herself to get angry, but not hurt. (After years of therapy, she is now allowing herself to feel sadness.) Anger is often a defense against sorrow.

Mothers who have said that they have never had any trouble with their children will nevertheless admit that the children do not show much emotion in the face of loss. Because the loss of a grandparent or a beloved pet can trigger memories of the first loss, children are often numbed by this and express very little, if any, affect. Their feelings go underground; they "numb out." This is often interpreted by the parents or others as the child's being callous or unfeeling, when he is actually warding off devastation. To feel this devastation, to reexperience the original loss is too painful, so the child denies the impact of the loss as a defense against psychological deterioration.

When my daughter was ten, my father died unexpectedly. They had shared a very close relationship and I knew that she was devastated by the death of her grandfather. She did cry and talk about it somewhat, but the most noticeable response was that of resignation and heightened vigilance, as if she knew that closeness meant inevitable loss and a subsequent need to defend against its happening again. She even said, "You see, Mom, I told you it was easier not to love in the first place." I replied, "Yes, love is a risk, because we can never be sure that the person we love will be around forever. But isn't it better that you had those ten years of love and closeness to Grandpa than to have missed them? It gave you and Grandpa both something special that, without the risk, you would have missed. I know that it was important to you both." Although she listened intently, I am not sure that she was convinced. As an adult, she can now look back on her relationship with her grandfather with fond memories, but for a long time the loss, the reopening of that wound, seemed almost unbearable.

"If You Leave, You're Out!"

Another manifestation of the trauma of abandonment is that of being unable or unwilling to allow anyone who is perceived to have abandoned the adoptee back into his life. Ginger says that she is stoic in the face of loss, and that she never knows what the real feeling is. She doesn't cry. "Tears and sadness don't come out, and anger is a 'flash in the pan.'" If people leave her, she will not allow them back into her life. "I tend to say 'fine,' if someone separates from me and leaves me. That's it! I shut the door on the person and I don't let them back in. It's like 'I dare you. You leave and that's it!'"

It doesn't seem to matter that the person could not have avoided the separation. Jennifer's best friend Alice left for Europe when her father was transferred, and Jennifer was inconsolable for days. She said that it was more than losing her best friend, it was like losing a part of herself. Yet when Alice returned two years later, Jennifer wasn't able to allow her into her life in the same way. She rationalized about it at the time, but she knows that it was really that she could not trust that Alice would not leave again, and she could not allow the vulnerability which she had allowed herself in the first place. She has not since been so attached to a girl or woman friend.

Hannah had a similar experience and said that she was able to tolerate the deaths of her grandparents all right, but she cannot tolerate the end of relationships. Jo Anne said that she "cut off" feelings of loss when her father died. In relationships, even short-term relationships, she has difficulty adjusting to separation or to being alone.

Fears of Abandonment Are Not Fantasies

Therapists write about the fantasies related to abandonment which cause adopted children to cling to adoptive parents or fantasize about a reunion with the birthmother. There is often a discounting of the importance of these fantasies or an implication that they are irrational. It should be noted that, although the fear of being abandoned by the adoptive parents might be fantasy, *there is a precedent for that fear in the original abandonment experience,* which may be felt only unconsciously. The fear, therefore, should not be perceived as irrational. One learns from experience, after all, and all adoptees have experienced abandonment.

Abandonment, to any child, is the greatest fear of all. There is nothing that can "shape up" a child so fast as a threat to "send him back where he came from" or to "let him see how he likes living someplace else." Even children who are abused by their parents have a deep sense of loyalty toward them and a fear of being separated from them.

In myth and fairy tale the theme of abandonment is dominant. Is it not possible that this fear hangs like the sword of Damocles over the heads of all adoptees all their lives, but about which they might not be consciously aware? I believe that it is possible, and that it is this unconscious fear which causes the anxiety experienced by so many adoptees. Although the adoptee might not be consciously aware of the fear of abandonment, which is then felt as free-floating anxiety, there is an attitude which can be readily discerned. It is a kind of watchfulness or cautious testing of the environment, which is called hypervigilance. At the infant stage, hypervigilance can be noticed by very observant nurses, social workers, or adoptive parents and is often described as awareness, alertness, or being a "live one." It may be, however, as I described earlier, an anxious response to abandonment and one way in which a relinquished child hopes to avoid a repeat of the abandonment experience.

Stealing and Hoarding

Another behavior which manifests in adopted children is stealing or hoarding. The child may steal or take money or food in a seemingly irrational concern about there not being enough "food." The precedent-forming experience has been that the "feeder" disappeared, resulting in a pervasive fear that he may some day have to be on his own and had better be prepared. The people from whom the child steals are those he likes or respects the most: his parents, siblings, teachers, or best friends. Some adoptees, reflecting upon this as adults, say that part of this is a feeling that they themselves had been stolen (which is easier to accept than the fact that their mothers gave them away), and that, therefore, stealing must be all right. It is a legitimate way to get what one feels one needs. And there is a tremendous reluctance to return that which was stolen, which is connected to the fear of being rejected or returned by the adoptive parents. "If I have to return the money, my parents might have to return me." If the parents can acknowledge this fear as a way of expressing an earlier experience and yet let the child know that the behavior cannot be tolerated, the anxiety level may be lowered and the need to hoard and steal diminished. Children need to know that they are understood, and they need help in understanding their own feelings and behaviors.

Control as a Foil to Loss

One of the ways in which children (and adults, too) try to prevent future losses is to try to be in absolute control of every situation. I mentioned in the Preface that at times my daughter's need to be in control seemed like a matter of life and death. Nothing I suggested, from what food to eat to which clothes to wear, was ever right. And yet, she could never really make up her own mind. Getting ready to go anywhere became a nightmare.

I hear similar stories from many, many adoptive parents. The simplest household decision or suggested deviation from routine becomes an immense struggle for control. It isn't just a matter of opinions or taste, it is a matter of survival. *The child was not in control of the situation at the beginning of his life, and look what happened!* It becomes intolerable to these children ever again to allow anyone else to be in control of their lives. They fight it at every turn. These struggles can be won by neither parent nor child, because if the parent gives up and allows the child to decide for himself, the issue then becomes, "You never help me," or "You don't really care." Parents often feel as if they are in a "Catch-22" situation.

The battle for control appears to the parents like obstinacy, which technically it is, but it emanates from a tremendous fear on the part of the child of another abandonment. That which looks to parents like hatred, rejection, or insolence has at the root of it an enormous dependency and need for acceptance, yet a lack of trust in those upon whom the child is supposed to depend. If the parents' need for acceptance rivals that of the child's, the problems become almost intolerable for everyone concerned. In the last part of the book I will talk about ways of defusing the inevitable fireworks which result from the issue of control.

For adoptees, the need to defend against the possibility of abandonment or other losses intrudes into almost every relationship, beginning with that of the adoptive mother and including their relationships to friends, lovers, and even themselves.

Summary

Our failure to acknowledge the devastation of separation from the birthmother on adopted children extends into many other areas of our society, where we routinely ignore or deny the impact of loss. Unresolved grief over some long-forgotten (or repressed) loss may be at the root of much of that which is considered clinical depression in our society.

While it is true that many grieving people need help, this help is not so much in the form of getting them through it quickly as it is in giving them permission to feel their loss and the time and means to process it. Most of these people are not sick or abnormal; they are people who are suffering as a result of society's ignorance, and its use of denial as a major defense against pain and paradox.

Although blaming the victim is often a phenomenon of trauma, (rape victims and battered women, for instance), being separated from their birthmothers and handed over to strangers in the adoption process is the only trauma where the victims are expected by the whole of society to be grateful. They are not grateful; they are grieving, and the original abandonment and loss are the sources of many other issues for the adoptee.

CHAPTER 7

Issues of Rejection, Trust, Intimacy, and Loyalty

There is a deep yearning inside me to have a lasting and meaningful relationship with someone, but it scares me, because if you let yourself get too close, you can't trust that you won't be abandoned again. That fear of rejection . . . The way I take care of this is to reject the other person first. They never have a chance!

—AN ADOPTEE

Difficulties in Relationships

When adult adoptees come in for psychotherapy, the usual presenting problem is difficulties in relationships. It is rare for an adoptee to come in and say, "I want to work on my adoption issues." When that does happen it is usually after he or she has been in treatment for years with little noticeable change. Then the conversation goes something like, "Well, I've worked on everything else, I guess I finally have to admit that my adoption might have something to do with what's going on." This is a very big step, because it means that the denial has been pierced. It also must be recognized that there is probably a great deal of guilt connected to letting that idea out of the depths of the unconscious and into the light of day.

At the mention of adoption, if the clinician is at all willing to accept its significance, he often assumes that there must have been something wrong with the adoptive parents (which may or may not be true) and, again, the issue of what happened *before* the child entered the family (unless there were multiple and/or abusive foster homes) is overlooked. In any case the abandonment and substitution of mothers is rarely considered a significant factor in what is going on for the adoptee.

And yet the experience of abandonment has a legacy which branches out into various other issues which affect adoptees to some degree in most of their significant relationships. The fear of abandonment does not leave an adoptee when he reaches adulthood, but can be seen in the way in which he conducts his relationships with important people in his life.

For people who have had a continuity from pre- to postnatal bonding, the original attachment and bonding experience and the appropriate separation from the mother at the proper time in one's development prepares one for many attachments and separations over and over throughout one's life. There may be a sense of missing someone if a loss is temporary, or a real sense of loss and sadness if a separation is permanent, but short separations or even important losses do not usually paralyze or cause panic. One can see a friend once every two years and rest assured that one is remembered and loved in the meantime. There is no sense that one might disappear from the friend's consciousness or that one might indeed just disappear. One can go on with life. Annihilation will not happen.

Yet for many adoptees, if they have not completely withdrawn emotionally, this is just the phenomenon they describe upon significant or even temporary separations and losses: panic and fear of annihilation. This panic and fear have nothing to do with the present circumstance, as difficult as it may be. Rather it has to do with the triggering of archaic memory traces of the original abandonment and the life-threatening experience that it was. Each impending or perceived threat of abandonment sets up a domino effect of other issues, which inhibits the normal ebb and flow of relationships—their establishment, deepening, or even their endings.

Issues of Rejection, Trust, Intimacy, and Loyalty

Some of these issues are fear of rejection, lack of trust, fear of intimacy, loyalty, shame and guilt, identity, and power or mastery and control. Although these issues will manifest in different ways and affect each person in varying degrees, it has been my observation that for those adoptees who are no longer in denial as a defense against true feelings all of these issues are present to some degree.

Now it might be said that these issues are present for everyone to some degree, not just for adoptees; but it is not enough to be aware of the issues. One also needs to ascertain and respect the etiology or cause, the experiences which brought about the issues. An adoptee who gets into treatment because of relationship issues will need to have his therapist recognize his issues of abandonment, fear of intimacy, and splitting (between good and bad) as having different causes from those of a person who is suffering, for instance, from certain personality disorders. This difference is not always respected by clinicians, to the detriment of the treatment process.

Having considered the effects of separation and loss, what about the other issues which are precipitated by that separation? Closely related to fear of abandonment is the fear of any type of rejection.

Fear of Rejection

Being wanted by my adoptive parents doesn't compare to being unwanted by my birthmother.
—AN ADOPTEE

The Bad-Baby Syndrome

The particular adoptee quoted above said that she didn't feel chosen, she felt rejected. A baby can't be chosen by one set of parents unless she has already been unchosen by the first set. Since it is hard to figure out what a tiny baby can *do* to become unchosen, it must

83

have been who she *was* that was rejected. This is the feeling reported by many adoptees, when they are able to put words to their very early feelings. The words are something like this: "A mother wouldn't give away a good baby, therefore I must have been a bad baby." This feeling of having an innate flaw carries over even into adulthood. This sets up adopted children for feelings of failure on every level, where every subsequent rejection, even the slightest one, simply reinforces their belief in their innate "badness."

One therapist, attempting to get through her patient's conviction that she had been (and still carried within her) a "bad baby" actually had the patient hold a baby and look carefully at it. She then asked, "How bad do you think this baby can be?" It was only then that the adoptee began to wonder about her long-held belief in her innate badness.

Relationships become dangerous, not only because one can't trust the people with whom one wants to relate, but also because they might find out about the "bad baby." This fear is exemplified by the hesitancy with which many adoptees get into relationships. The difficulties begin in childhood, where they find themselves isolated and having few friends. They sometimes develop a state of acute anxiety with accompanying feelings of isolation, unreality, and alienation often attributed to maternal failure in infancy. To the adoptee it doesn't necessarily seem like maternal failure, but "baby failure." Glenda, who suffered from asthma most of her life, often felt as if she were suffocating. She said that she associated that feeling of suffocation with having been abandoned and feeling that she didn't have a right to exist.

The Losers and Stoners

Valerie isolated herself as a child by avoiding everyone with the exception of one friend. She describes herself as always feeling like an "awful person." As a student, she only associated with people "at the bottom of the list" so far as popularity was concerned, because that was where she felt she belonged.

Mary Beth says that she was well-liked but didn't feel popular. She recalls being "a loner, a melancholy kid." As a child, she would show off for adults, but wouldn't mix with other children. As an adolescent she "ran around" with the popular crowd, but felt "like a fraud."

Norma says that people like her but she doesn't trust getting close. She is always nice to people, "because you never know who your birthmother is." She says of her youth that she didn't "do" pot or other drugs, but nevertheless always associated with the groups known as the "losers and stoners." That was where she felt she belonged. Those were the people who would accept her.

Jody, who said that he loved school and pushed himself into being an overachiever, nevertheless had difficulty with peers. "I didn't work well with people my own age. I tended to just shut myself off." This feeling of "shutting themselves off" to avoid a possible rejection can, perhaps, be summed up by Mary Beth, who said, "I will set the scene so that, hopefully, I won't be rejected, or it won't even come near that. So I won't have to go through that rejection. . . . I just don't want to take the chance that they are going to reject me in *any* way, whether it be small, medium, or large." For many adoptees one way of assuring that they won't be rejected is to associate with the "losers and stoners" of life.

Testing Out

For many of these adoptees the fear of rejection and their need to defend against further rejections causes them to withdraw and isolate themselves. For others, however, there is a tendency to push for rejection, even though this is the opposite of what they want. Johanna lists the greatest fear throughout her life as that of not being loved or liked. She constantly tests people, beginning with her parents, to see if they will reject her. She will get superficially close to people, but never really lets them know her. She thinks that her feelings of unworthiness go back to her initial rejection and have become a pattern in her life.

This fear of rejection sometimes sets up a counterphobic reaction of rejecting others before one is rejected—sabotaging relationships. In other words, instead of the Golden Rule of "Do unto others as you would have them do unto you," the rule of these adoptees is "Do unto others first that which you fear they are going to do to you." This is often what happens in the relationship with the adoptive mother, where she is tested over and over again to see if she is going to reject the child. The constant anxiety caused by the expectation of her eventual rejection and the child's need to let her know how he feels creates a cycle of rejective behavior between mother and child, which is destructive to their self-esteem and to their relationship.

It is not just the adoptive mother who experiences this testing behavior. Alison says, "I can stay in destructive relationships all right, because that is what I feel I deserve. But if I accidentally find myself with a really good person, I always do something to destroy it. I don't do this on purpose. I don't even realize it until it is over."

However, other people do realize their tendency to destroy relationships. "I know that I'm setting out to sabotage myself, but I can't seem to help it," Joni says. "It seems to be coming from outside myself. Every once in awhile I catch myself, but it is usually only a delay, a reprieve. The next time I'll really do it. The next time he'll leave."

This testing-out or rejecting behavior is often an enigma for the friends and partners of adoptees. As described by the adoptee at the beginning of this chapter, many of their friends feel as if they haven't been given a chance. They are at a loss to know what is going on or what to do about it: "Joan really mystifies me. She will just finish telling me how much I mean to her, them BOOM, she says something which she knows hurts me or she'll go out with another guy or something. I don't get it."

Issues of Rejection, Trust, Intimacy, and Loyalty

Rejection and Work

One of the problems often expressed to me by parents of adolescent adoptees is their reluctance to get jobs, which is perceived by the parents as laziness. I believe that there is more to it than that. When asked to talk about why they find it so difficult to look for work, adoptees will often say that they might not get the job. In other words, they might be rejected by the interviewer or boss, who for one reason or another wants another person for that job. Now while many people would just go to the next interview and keep pursuing it until a job was found, the adoptee will often feel paralyzed by that initial rejection. It is felt, not just as a failure to have the necessary skills or training for the job, but as a rejection of his basic person. *He* was not good enough for the job. He was a failure. This makes going out and facing the next interview seem like a monumental task. A simple acknowledgment by the parents that they understand what is going on, even if the adoptee denies it (which he may do, because he is not always consciously aware of it), may help him feel understood or at least uncriticized and more willing to try again. Just chastising him for being lazy is *not* going to help.

The fear of rejection in the workplace is often accompanied by a fear of success or an inability to believe in one's competency or expertise. There is a kind of self rejection of one's own talents and capabilities, which sometimes results in a sabotaging of one's success. Or else, in the paradoxical way these things work for adoptees, there is a need to be perfect, to be the best, to get one more Ph.D. to prove that one has a right to exist.

Barney says that the fear of rejection gets worse with age, but that he has learned to handle it better. This is connected to his feelings of unworthiness, which he knows intellectually are unfounded: "That's probably caused more trouble for me in my life than anything else. If I ever once just believed that I was special! God has given me so many gifts, and so many people have had so much enjoyment from my music, and I'm still not believing it most of the time."

The fear that he is unworthy makes the adoptee so very sensitive to criticism or the slightest hint of rejection that many people feel at a loss to know how to keep from triggering it. It interferes with relationships, jobs, and school, and often brings about the very outcome which the adoptee fears.

Issues of Trust and Intimacy

The issues of trust and intimacy are closely related to those of abandonment and rejection. There is such a fluid movement among these issues that it is difficult to separate them. The adoptees' lack of trust in the permanency of relationships brings about a distrust of closeness or intimacy and a need for distancing. At the same time there is a yearning for the very thing which is feared.

The confusion about what the true feeling is was expressed by Janice, who said that she has difficulty in all aspects of relationships and can't always distinguish between trust and attachment: "If I'm feeling unworthy, it is going to be difficult to trust anybody, because I don't believe that they can really like me, because I don't feel that I'm very likable; therefore, I am not going to be very intimate. I'm afraid that they are going to reject me." She either doesn't allow herself to attach in the first place or she has difficulty leaving even bad relationships. She feels like a "real bad person" if she leaves—or even if he does. She always assumes that the fault is hers. She doesn't want to reject other people. She would rather be rejected herself than "do that" to someone else. She is used to "dealing with" rejection and can "handle it." She feels that her problem in separating is based on the loss that she feels.

After one especially painful loss, Janice decided to "put my feelings in a box" and not feel. This lasted for eight years, until she had strong feelings for a therapist. Most of the relationships to which she referred were those with men. She is not sure how she would react to the loss of a woman friend, because, except for the therapist, she hasn't had close relationships with women for long enough to see "how that works." She is just beginning to have close relationships with a few selected women, but it feels "very scary." I chose to explore Janice's experience more fully, because she, as a result of her therapy and much introspection, had reached a point where she was able to articulate that at which many adoptees can only hint.

Distrust of the Feminine

As it has been shown in the often tumultuous relationship between the adoptee and the adoptive mother, women are often seen as abandoners, unworthy of trust. This belief extends to other women as well. Although the "one best friend" of most adoptees is usually of the same sex as themselves, the rest of their friends and acquaintances tend to be, for both sexes, boys or men. There is a general feeling of not trusting girls or women, of not being accepted by them, or of feeling generally uncomfortable around them.

After years of therapy, Vonita is just beginning to trust her relationships with women: "I always thought they didn't like me, that they'd like other people better, that it was probably easier for them to be closer to somebody else."

Wanda volunteered that she has difficulty believing that people really like her " . . . especially women. If women like me, I freak out." In the last year or two she has met some women who genuinely like her. "I know they like me, and it just kills me. And that means more to me than any relationship I've ever had," and she began to cry.

Judy, who rationalized her preference for men by believing that she enjoyed talking about ideas (perhaps safer than talking about feelings?), now says that she prefers being around women. She still fears that they will disappear from her life, however. This same fear was voiced by Alison, who said that she is constantly surprised when her women friends remember her and like her. She cannot retain this idea when she is not with them.

Difficulties in Separating

Many adoptees find it difficult to attach or allow closeness in relationships because of the fear that each new relationship, *like the very first relationship*, will not last. Bill describes it as "being very cautious before allowing closeness," so that he won't have to face an abandonment. He doesn't attach very readily, but once attached he has a difficult time separating.

Separating seems to be an even greater problem than attaching. Once a relationship is established many adoptees do not want to separate, even when the relationship proves unsatisfactory. Trudy had been in what she described as a "real sick" marriage with an older man for several years. The relationship seemed to her more like a parent/child relationship than a marriage. Even though she was very unhappy, she could not leave the relationship until she had undergone some intense therapy.

Meredith says, "I'm afraid to be open about my feelings and never tell my friends everything—you know, like some women do. I don't want to get too close. But when I do attach at all, I can't let go. I mourn losses for a long time."

Distrusting the Self

Distrust is evident, not only in the permanency of relationships, but in the goodness of self, as described previously. This lack of self-esteem or self-worth is intricately intertwined with the lack of trust and fear of intimacy described by many of the adoptees with whom I have spoken. I guess it was best summed up by Denise, who said, "If my own mother couldn't love me, who can?" Reassuring her that her mother did love her isn't helpful, because it brings up the non sequitur: "Your mother really loved you, so she gave you up." This may make sense to the adult adoptee on the intellectual level, but it doesn't make any sense at all to the baby who resides within that adult.

Loyalty

Regardless of the issues of rejection, trust, and intimacy which emanate from the original relinquishment, and even in spite of the eventual feelings of rage which may arise, there seems to be a sense of loyalty stemming from the profound connection between biological mother and child. B. J. Lifton, who has written extensively about adoption, once told me she feels that the difficulty in bonding with the adoptive mother is not so much a matter of trust as it is a matter of loyalty to that first mother. While I disagreed with her at first, I now believe that both of the issues of trust and loyalty are present in the dilemma for the child.

Divided Loyalty

On the personal level, once I was able to give up the idea that I was going to be *the* mother, that I could take the place of the biological mother, there was a kind of relaxation in my daughter's attitude towards me. I never really expressed this to her in words, but there was a way in which I must have conveyed the idea to her that she no longer had to defend that place in her heart against intrusion from me. I don't want to give the impression that this was easy for me to do. It was only after years of therapy and soul-searching that I was able to have such a transpersonal attitude in my relationship with my beloved daughter. She is my daughter, but I am not her only mother.

The loyalty toward the birthmother is only one part of the picture. There is at the same time a sense of loyalty to the adoptive parents, which often enters into the decision about whether or not to search. It is often assumed by the adoptee, sometimes correctly and sometimes incorrectly, that the adoptive parents will feel rejected or replaced by any relationship between their child and his or her biological parents. This sense of loyalty does not always disappear with the assurance that the adoptive parents understand the need to search and will even assist in implementing it. Just as there seems to be a great deal of trouble believing that a parent can equally love more than one child (everyone wants to be the best-loved child), there seems to be difficulty in believing that a child can love two sets of parents. This disbelief may be present in the child as well as in the parents. Michelle said to me, "If my parents are willing to share me with my birth parents, maybe that means that they don't really love me." This wasn't the only time I heard adoptees express ambivalent feelings about their adoptive parents' willingness to share their child. It seems as if for some adoptees the *fear* that their parents would object might, instead, be a *wish* that they would object—a proof of their parents' devotion.

Loyalty to the Lost Child

Birthmothers also have a sense of loyalty to that lost child. There is a high rate of secondary infertility among them (perhaps as high as 40%). Those who never conceive again say things such as: "I couldn't be unfaithful to him. I have a hard time even holding my little nephew." "I felt unworthy to be a mother after giving my firstborn away." "It would be disloyal to her to have another baby. She will always be my only child." There is so much pain and guilt connected to the surrendering of the child that many birthmothers give up their rights to motherhood.

Divided loyalty, which is quite visible in step-families, is also present in adoptive families, although it is more covert. This makes the relationship to the adoptive parents, the birth parents, and to others very confusing and conflicted for adoptees. The adoptive mother often feels like the "wicked stepmother," an interloper in the connection and loyalty between her child and his first mother (although most adoptive mothers are not apt to put it this way). Whereas the birthmother may feel guilty for having given up her baby, the adoptive mother feels guilty for somehow failing to adequately take her place. *The child feels guilty for having been born.*

CHAPTER 8

Issues of Guilt and Shame, Power and Control, Identity

Guilt and Shame

Guilt is another issue for adoptees. Actually, while guilt is often predominant for both birth and adoptive mothers, it is probably shame which is felt most by adoptees. What is the difference between them? The easiest way to understand this is to think of the difference between doing and being. One may feel guilty for what one has done or caused, but shame for who one is. Shame is connected to an adoptee's belief that he or she is unlovable: He is ashamed of who he is.

Guilt is not always inappropriate; in fact it is often helpful in one's holding to one's moral code. If one hurts someone, for instance, it is appropriate to feel guilty about it and hopefully refrain from doing it again. Guilt is inappropriate, however, when the person feeling guilty has had no real control over whatever happened: children feeling guilty about their parents' divorce, for example.

Shame, on the other hand, is a completely useless feeling, because it means that a person is ashamed of the very core of his being. Adoptees are quite familiar with this feeling. It is the feeling of being the "bad baby," the baby who wasn't good enough to keep. The adoptive parents' assurance that he was chosen, that he is special, that they truly love and want him is to no avail. Jeannette put it this way, "Oh yeah, my adoptive parents said that they loved me, but let's face it, who can really love a reject?" Or as Bill said, "I was a throw-away. Who's gonna love me?"

Part of this feeling of shame has to do with the feeling of incompleteness which follows the premature separation from the birthmother. Something is missing. There is a feeling that he is disabled or handicapped. He is not whole or wholesome. He is defective, impaired, fragmented. Often the search for the mother is an attempt to heal this defect, mend the wound, perfect the imperfect.

Biological children raised in the same home with an adopted brother or sister often feel as if they are living with a handicapped person who needs 90% of the attention. They often wish that they themselves were handicapped, not only to gain some of that attention, but also because they feel guilty for not having been adopted. They have ambivalent feelings of compassion and anger about the intense feelings and outrageous behavior which are generated by the adoptee's anxiety, yet feel helpless to do anything about it. Parents also feel helpless, because it seems that no matter what they do, it is wrong. It seems like a Catch-22 situation, with no one the winner.

The "cure" seems to make the pain worse. The more the parents demonstrate affection, the higher the anxiety of the adoptee, and the more acting out he does. There is no way for others to convince adoptees that they are wonderful, lovable, beautiful people. If they get gentle, steadfast love and constancy of availability from those who love them (which includes absolutely *no* threat of abandonment), they may begin to trust in the *possibility* of their own goodness. But the only sure way for adoptees to rid themselves of shame is for them to work

95

it through for themselves. It is not enough for adoptees to gain acceptance from others; ultimately they must learn to love and accept themselves.

Power or Mastery and Control

Adoptee as Victim

Closely related to guilt and shame is control. To be guilty of something means that one has or had some control over the situation. One could have done something differently. Yet even though adoptees tend to feel innately responsible for their own relinquishment, there is a paradoxical feeling of having been a victim. This, then, implies a need for someone to blame. Adoptees vacillate back and forth between blaming themselves for not having been good enough to keep to having a feeling of helplessness and undifferentiated anger for having been so manipulated. This ambivalence is sometimes misinterpreted by therapists when adoptees are in treatment, and seen as an excuse for not taking responsibility for themselves. They are sometimes seen as using their adoptive status as a rationalization for conflicts which arise with parents, making resolution of the conflict impossible.

While it is true that seeing adoption as the only issue may cause parents and children to overlook some obvious interpersonal conflicts, it is important to keep in mind that adoptees *are* victims of manipulation of the gravest kind: the severing of their tie to the birthmother and their biological roots. The feeling of being a victim is not just a fantasy, but a reality. Being abandoned often leaves one with a permanent feeling of being at the mercy of others.

The fact that the child does not consciously remember the substitution of mothers does not diminish the impact of that experience. In fact the inability to consciously remember the experience may make the impact even more devastating and perplexing. One adoptee said that the most important thing I ever told her was that feelings have memories. That statement validated a variety of emotions and beliefs, the sources of which she could not trace, but which were very strong and persistent. One such belief was that of being a victim, about which she often felt guilty. Understanding the possible source of her sense of being a victim may have been the first step toward her being able to feel more in control of her life and less a victim.

Having been manipulated at the beginning of their lives makes some adoptees manipulative and controlling. Families of acting-out adoptees will know what I am talking about. There seems to be an almost desperate need to be in control at all times. Some adoptees control situations by becoming isolated and detached, while others are more overt in their controlling mechanisms. In the first case there seems to be a need to avoid being in a situation again which might trigger rejection and possible abandonment, while in the other there seems to be a need to relieve anxiety by getting the inevitable abandonment over with. In both cases the adoptee feels like a victim desperately trying to gain some control over his situation. Parents and clinicians should not dismiss the feeling of victimization on the part of the adoptee as a rationalization and a means of avoiding the resolution of conflicts with his parents. They should, instead, first acknowledge the child's feelings, then go on to the interpersonal problem.

Lashing out against the adoptive parents is a way for the adoptee to try to externalize his inner shame. "I don't know why I was always so angry at my parents. When I think about it, they never did anything to make me that angry. It was as if I was trying to rid myself of something inside me and the only way I could do it was to put it on them. That doesn't make any sense, does it?" asked Andrew. Yes, it makes sense in light of his experience. Yet at the same time, it is destructive to the relationship, because the parents also feel victimized. In working with adoptive families, it seems to be tremendously helpful for the adoptive parents to understand the source of their child's anger, because instead of becoming defensive, they can acknowledge feelings.

Life Isn't Fair!

Feeling like a victim sometimes has a paralyzing effect on an adoptee, because even though he tries to control his environment, he still doesn't feel as if he is in control of his life. His striving to be complete was disrupted by someone taking over his life and altering it forever. This feels unnatural and may stymie the natural continuity of developmental tasks, such as learning the relationship between cause and effect or, more personally, that his actions have consequences for which he is responsible. While the rest of the family may feel as if the adoptee (if he is the acting-out type) is controlling the whole family, taking up everyone's space, and requiring 90% of the attention, the adoptee himself may feel completely at the mercy of circumstances beyond his control. He may have feelings that life isn't fair, or that he really can't help what he is doing.

Adoptees often have poor frustration tolerance or impulse control. This means that the slightest thing, such as difficulty in tying their shoes or finding an object, may make them inappropriately angry and reactive. It also means that they lack the inner brakes on impulses that might normally be expected for their age group. In other words it is easier for them to control the rest of the family than it is for them to control themselves. One way that they do this is by making the whole family give in to their behavior in order to avoid conflict over mundane things. It is difficult for them to take responsibility for themselves, especially as children and adolescents. It isn't a question of mind over matter, as many parents suspect. Adoptees really *don't* feel as if they have any control in their lives. They really *do* feel like victims, so they react angrily to that feeling of helplessness.

If they are the compliant, "walking-on-eggshells" type, however, they may appear to be overly responsible. Rather than it being due to a healthy integration of the relationship between cause and effect in the normal sense, however, this overly responsible behavior may be a response to anxiety. It may be due to the feeling that the original cause of their abandonment was that they were defective, so that in effect they now have to be perfect. As Rick said, "I knew I had to be a better person than the one who was given away."

As adults, adoptees sometimes find themselves to be perennial students, never quite figuring out what they want to do in life. Often even the idea of applying for a job or going to an interview fills them with dread, as has been mentioned before. The fear of rejection paralyzes them, leaving them again feeling a failure. One mother said, "Alan used to tell us constantly that he couldn't wait until he was 18 so he could move out. Now he's 23 and is still here. He lies in bed until noon, always promising to go out and look for a job. What can we do? We don't want him to feel like we're abandoning him."

This is, indeed, a dilemma for families who are actually aware of the delicate balance between abandonment and the need to push for their children to grow up and take responsibility. The adoptee will often vacillate in his response to the parents by either telling them that they can't run his life or accusing them of not caring. Children who do leave home often do so as a defense against being kicked out, rather than as an appropriate response to the current stage of their developmental process. Even for those who make a smooth transition out of their families, there is often a feeling that something was left undone: "Sure, I went away to college, just like my friends; but there was always this nagging feeling that I forgot something, that I'd left something unfinished. I can't really describe it, but it just feels incomplete—you know, like forgetting to brush your teeth before going to bed—but stronger than that. I don't know. . . . "

Before one can truly separate, one must first connect, and I think that for many adoptees, the inability to really bond with their adoptive mothers leaves them feeling as if they are not yet ready to separate. And if they are not ready to separate, how can they be autonomous, independent, adult beings? Being adopted sometimes makes an adoptee feel as if he is perpetually a child. As B.J. Lifton says, "Who has ever heard of an adopted adult?" The adoptee didn't choose the circumstances of his life, and he feels as if he is powerless over them even as an adult.

Parents often hear their children saying, "It isn't my fault," "I couldn't help it," or "I didn't do it," even in the face of overwhelming evidence to the contrary. And, although it may be evident to the parent that the child was responsible for what happened, the child probably actually feels as if it were out of his control. In the last part of this book I will have some suggestions for adoptive parents to facilitate a balance between the security of necessary boundaries and a child's having some sense of control in his life.

Identity

Adolescence is a difficult time in the lives of parents and their children whether adopted or not, but it seems especially difficult for those children who have no sense of their history. During adolescence, when everyone is searching for his own identity, it becomes more difficult for the adoptee to deny the fact that he has no long-term history with the people by whom he is being reared. Not only does he find it difficult to identify his own personal history with that of his family, but he experiences a great deal of conflict around the idea of searching for that personal history. For the hitherto compliant adoptee, this may be the first time he becomes aware of his deep feelings about his relinquishment and adoption.

The lack of personal history is a handicap for the adoptee because of the importance of knowing one's past before planning for the future. In an attempt to do this, some adoptees tend to identify with their perception of the birth parents, especially the mother, who is sometimes perceived as young and promiscuous or a member of royalty. The idea that she was probably an ordinary, vulnerable, and confused young person, a great deal like the adoptee himself, is not usually one of the fantasies he has about his birthmother.

Because of the dearth of information about his own history, the adoptee often has a more stressful adolescence than his non-adopted counterpart. That profound separation of his biological sense of

100

himself and his inability to identify with either of his adoptive parents may prompt some adoptees to act out destructively during adolescence, even if they had previously been compliant. This often astonishes their adoptive parents, who had thought that their child had made a good adjustment. The parents often feel betrayed by their previously docile child and unable to cope with the situation.

Many adoptees and their parents end up feeling rejected and hurt, with the children often leaving home prematurely. One parent explained, "Dodie was always such a loving daughter. I thought we had a wonderful relationship. Now she has just disappeared. Why is she doing this to us? Was she just acting all those years? I feel so hurt, angry and betrayed. But I'd give anything if she'd just come back. I miss her so much!" Dodie's sister had been the acting-out child, so until adolescence Dodie had been compliant and acquiescent. Then, with her sister out of the picture, she began to act out her own pain, which took her parents completely by surprise. This is a story I have heard many times.

The reasons vary for leaving home prematurely. Some adoptees leave as a result of having been kicked out by parents unable to cope with the rebellion, which often becomes intolerable. The adoptees themselves have some sense of the outrageousness of their behavior, yet they seem unable to stop themselves. Too often misguided clinicians advise the parents to send the child to an adolescent treatment center or special school. They are completely unaware of the significance this solution has on the child. Whereas in some cases this may be the last resort and only thing to do, on the psychological level it only reinforces and exacerbates the abandonment issue for adoptees. These institutions rarely address abandonment issues in a manner which is healing to the adoptee.

Many adoptees, in anticipation of being kicked out of the home, leave—rejecting their parents before their parents have a chance to reject them. Ron said, "I always had this feeling of impending doom at home. Nothing was ever said, but I felt like they were going to kick me out. When I was sixteen I left home to live with a girl friend. But then I kept going back, then leaving again. I finally left for the last time at nineteen. My parents and I talk to each other, but we aren't really close. I don't know why."

Other adoptees leave because they no longer want to do what these parents, to whom they are not really related, want them to do. "They don't know me. They don't understand me. They aren't really my parents. They were always trying to control me, like they thought I was going to do something terrible or something. I just had to get out." In all of these cases, the resulting alienation is felt by both child and parents and is difficult to heal—not impossible, however, as I will discuss later.

There are some adoptees who deny being curious about their origins. This is seen by some professionals as an attempt to avoid upsetting the adoptive parents who want to maintain the illusion of a "natural" family. Some adoptive parents have a need to deny the adoption, or if not the adoption, the effect of the adoption on their children. Yet the fantasy of being a natural family is constantly being undermined by the absence of any biological relationship, such as physical features, interests, talents, or personality traits. "I never looked like anybody in my family. I've always wanted to meet someone who looked like me," Alice explained. Many adolescent pregnancies are attempts by adoptees to have someone biologically connected to them, "someone who looks like me."

The loss of the thread of family continuity, a deep identification with his ancestors whose genes are stamped into every cell of his body, contributes to the sense of insecurity felt by the adoptee. No matter how competent and loving the adoptive mother, the child shares no genetic history with her. He is deprived of that primitive relationship with the mother with whom he did share that history.

Adoptees are sometimes preoccupied with existential concerns. Being disconnected from his genetic heritage and randomly placed in another milieu causes him to lose any sense of the rightness of things.

Rather, he feels that life is purposeless, chaotic, and irrational, without order or meaning. This causes difficulties in his spiritual life, and poses problems in making significant choices, such as a career or a mate. The wish to search for birth parents becomes a means by which he may attempt to end the chaos, alienation, and isolation which result from the break in his genealogical history. Often the death of an adoptive parent or the birth of his own biological child will bring on an even deeper sense of genealogical bewilderment and a wish to search for birth parents.

The search for identity, which commonly takes place during adolescence and early adulthood, is a time of conflict and dissent for most parents and their children. For adoptees, however, there is the added complication of not having any genealogical connection to the people who reared them. Even if they want to identify with their adoptive parents, the personality traits which they inherited from their birth parents may make this very difficult. One clinician put it this way: "Adoptees have a Swiss-cheese identity—there are lots of holes in it." When physical appearance, personality, and ethnicity or culture are also different, each of these aspects makes identity with the adoptive parents that much more difficult.

This lack of personal identity precludes having a sense of belonging to the greater society. The question becomes, on a more global scale, "Where do I fit in?" One adoptee was telling me about a Star Trek episode (or two episodes) in which a child is born to people from another planet. The child's mother dies and the father returns to his native planet, leaving the child behind on Earth, where he doesn't feel as if he fits in because he is an alien. In the second episode, when he does return to his native planet, he doesn't feel as if he fits in there either. That describes the feeling of many adoptees even after they have found their birth parents. They do not fit in with their adoptive families with whom they share few personality traits, nor do they fit in with their birth families who may have been living in an entirely different environment. A great deal of understanding from everyone concerned is needed to help heal the feeling of alienation.

In my own personal experience with my daughter, one of the most wonderful aspects of having her in my life (besides just the fact of her *being*) is that she drew me out of my complacency. I was one of those adoptive parents who didn't believe I needed therapy. After all I was very functional and effective in all areas of my life (until I met failure in dealing with my daughter's pain). What I discovered about myself is that I was operating on only about two or three of my eight cylinders: Whole aspects of my personality were hidden and unused. Because I believe that we all have suffered "nicks to the soul," as one of my psych profs called them, I also believe that adoptive parents need to address their own issues in trying to help their children. What I discovered were many facets of my personality, which might have been undiscovered had Gisèle not forced me to take a look at myself. We are actually more alike now than we were when she was a child, not because she became like me, but because I allowed the more extraverted parts of my own personality to blossom as a result of being so closely involved with her. My therapy helped, of course, because it allowed me to feel more at home with myself, less narrow in my outlook. If adoptive parents are bogged down by their own inflexible world view and need a shot in the arm, paying attention to the true personality of their child may give them that boost into new dimensions of their own personalities. I would urge adoptive parents to foster the true personalities of their children (which is different from behavior caused by pain), so that they, too, may become open to new possibilities, less restricted and inflexible. It can be like opening a door to a brand new world.

Summary

The primary or core issues for adoptees are abandonment and loss. From those two issues the issues of rejection, trust, intimacy, loyalty, guilt and shame, power and control, and identity emanate. These issues are intertwined and fluid for most adoptees, yet are probably present even in those who seem "well-adjusted."

Part of the problem is getting through the denial in both adoptees and their parents about the differences between adoptive and so-called "natural" families. The first step for all triad members is to assess the level of awareness they have about adoption issues; in other words, the myths and stereotypes vs. reality. None of these issues can be addressed successfully unless they are also addressed honestly. The depth of the pain and the many issues caused by that pain are not easy to face, but for healing to begin doing so is essential. Parents, if they are honest in their perceptions about their child, can, with help from a professional, be tremendously effective in facilitating healing in their child. The next part of the book deals with this healing.

PART THREE

The Healing

I have presented my theory that all adoptees suffer a primal wound as a result of their separation from the first mother. I have also related some of the ways in which this wound might manifest as adoptees grow from childhood into adulthood. The questions now become: What are we to do with this information? Is adoption something to be avoided? And if it cannot be avoided, what should be done differently?

I believe that life is a paradox and that in order to avoid becoming frustrated and disillusioned, we have to accept this paradox (and perhaps even rejoice in it). We have to accept that life is not made up of absolutes: black or white, dark or light, fair or unfair, but that in all aspects of life one will find elements of both black *and* white and myriad shades of gray in between.

The answer to the difficulties with adoption is not to deny them, ignore them, or to do away with adoption in order to avoid them. The answer is to acknowledge those difficulties, live with that reality, and learn how to deal with it. Anyone who has grown up in a family knows that there are problems involved in being in such a relationship; yet we don't do away with families. Adoptive families have some different realities from biological families which must be acknowledged, understood, and dealt with.

There is a great deal of healing which needs to be done. It needs to be acknowledged that there is a wound, that the wound causes pain, and that this pain has an impact on all members of the adoption triad. The attitude of society and many clinicians that there is no difference between adoptive and biological families helps none of the people involved, because it discounts legitimate feelings. It negates the complexity and additional burdens placed upon the adoptive family unit, and the feelings of adoptees and birth parents. It offers no empathic understanding to the adoptees (who are expected to be grateful for being in such a nice family), to the adoptive parents (who are sometimes accused of just not loving or caring enough or they would not be having problems), or to the birthmothers (who are told that they made their choice, so they shouldn't complain or search).

The idea of a wound caused by an infant's being separated from its biological mother is not an easy idea to accept, because it implies that there is no way around this wound, no pat answers or magical solutions. It implies that *all* adopted children suffer from this wound, and that although there are certain criteria for evaluating the symptoms of the wound, different adoptees will respond to these manifestations differently. While it is certainly true that the wound cannot be entirely healed, it is hoped that there are ways in which it can at least be mitigated.

Healing must take place within various contexts: within the adoptive family, as adoptive parents learn ways in which to deal with their child's feelings, as well as their own; within healing support groups for each part of the triad—adoptee, birth parents, and adoptive parents, where each can seek support from others who have had the same experience and feelings; among triad members in the reunion process, where each part of the triad can learn to understand and empathize with one another's feelings; and finally, within society as a whole, as people become more and more aware of the impact of separating babies from their mothers, and understanding and helpful to those who are involved in that process.

Loss is paramount in the understanding of what is going on with each member of the adoption triad. The adoptee is feeling the loss of the birthmother, the birthmother is feeling the loss of her child, and the adoptive parents are feeling loss of their fertility and genetic continuity. None is able to grieve, sometimes because the feelings are so repressed or denied as to make them inaccessible; other times because society ignores their grief and thinks that the adoptee and adoptive parents should feel lucky, and that the birthmother made her choice and should get on with her life. As I said before, ours is not a society which understands loss very well. Adoption is seen as a happy event, which calls for celebration. And this may be true, at least for the adoptive parents; but it is also true that there is loss involved for everyone, loss which needs to be mourned. Loss which is not mourned can be debilitating, leaving one feeling at the mercy of unexplainable and unpredictable feelings. Understanding, acceptance, empathy, and communication are the keys to the beginning of healing.

CHAPTER 9

In the Best Interest of the Child

If anything in this book has made sense so far, then it will be apparent that psychologically what is truly *in the best interest of the child* is keeping babies and their mothers together. When that is not possible, then other measures must be taken to ensure that those children who have to be separated from their mothers are given the best chance in life. Too often we try to do what the adoptive parents, birth parents, social workers, or attorneys want, without ever considering the psychological impact those ideas or actions will have on the child. *Adoption should serve the children who need parents, not the childless couples who seek children.* If a child really does have to be separated from his mother, how should we proceed?

In the Beginning. . . .

There is a growing trend in this country toward what is called independent, open adoptions. This is seen as better than the secrecy and lack of genetic information which agency adoptions have provided in the past. Besides providing the child with a sense of his genetic history, it can also provide him with the possibility for some kind of relationship with his birthmother. Despite the advantages, many problems within this system are beginning to surface.

On the one hand, open adoptions give the birthmother more control over her child's destiny. This should have a calming effect on her during her pregnancy. As a relationship of trust begins to build between the adoptive and birth parents and they become more comfortable with one another, the birthmother's anxiety about the future of her baby may diminish, creating a more positive intrauterine climate for the fetus. On the other hand, there may be a feeling of obligation on the part of the birthmother to hand over her infant to the adoptive parents (who have become her friends), when at the moment of truth (birth) she may, in fact, decide that she can't give up her baby. The pressure upon her may be even greater if the adoptive parents take an active part in the birthing process, such as the adoptive mother acting as coach for the biological mother.

Sometimes there is a kind of ritual handing over of the baby with candles and soft-spoken words. There was a time when I was all in favor of this, because I felt that the love and trust between the two sets of parents would penetrate the preconscious being of the infant. After talking to many birthmothers and adoptees, however, I have changed my mind about this. The ritual/ceremony may make the two sets of parents feel better at the time (although one glance at the birthmother's face, usually reveals more agony than peace for her), but it will do nothing to soften the trauma for the child of separation from his biological mother. Many adolescent and adult adoptees have told me that they actually feel physically ill when seeing these cere-monies on television. They have described these rituals as "sick," "inhuman," "grotesque," "gross," "human sacrifice," and "ritual sacrifice." Although some adoptees admit that the intent may be good, not one adoptee with whom I've spoken felt positive about these rituals. (Others have a low opinion of the intent as well.)

In the Best Interest of the Child

The Need for a Conscious Decision

Doing what is in the best interest of the child necessitates there being an honest evaluation on the part of the birthmother about her feelings and situation. Many birthmothers are in almost total denial about how giving up their babies is going to affect them. Until that baby is born, he hasn't always become a reality to the mother. Her ultimate choice must be a conscious one, a true choice based upon honest information (educational and intuitive). This would involve impartial pre- and postnatal counseling, and time with her baby alone. It means that the birthmother would be allowed to give birth without the pressure which the physical presence of the adoptive parents in the delivery room would place upon her. Having the adoptive parents in the delivery room may be just as coercive as the pressures which are brought to bear by some agencies, attorneys, or independent adoption centers. She may have a hard time telling them that she just cannot relinquish her child. Or if she does, she may feel guilty about disappointing them. She needs to know that any guilt she may have towards the adopting parents may be insignificant compared to that which she may later feel toward the child should she decide to relinquish.

The adopting parents, no matter how much they want a baby, must also understand the implications for the baby if he is separated from his biological mother. The instinct to parent is powerful, and there is nothing wrong with admitting that this is the reason they want to adopt. It is much better to be honest about the yearning to be a parent than to proclaim some altruistic hocus-pocus about rescuing the child from some unknown, terrible fate. But no matter how much pain the prospective parents are in or how much they want a baby, satisfying one's desire to parent should not come at the expense of the welfare of the child.

Most adoptive parents never consider that the substitution of mothers could be harmful for the child. Why should they? No one has really suggested it. Their intent is good, but their understanding is lacking. No one has come right out and said in plain language that the child would be traumatized by being separated from his biological mother, and that, except in obvious cases, the best interest of the child may be better served by keeping him with her. If a birthmother changes her mind and wants to keep her baby, the prospective parents should not try to talk her out of it. A baby is not a commodity to be bargained for, and the biological mother owes nothing to the prospective adoptive parents. Yet she often feels exploited by them and by the attorneys who work for them. Her first obligation is to do what is best for her child.

The Flip Side of Exploitation

The issue of exploitation also comes up in regard to the biological mother's own attitudes toward the whole procedure of adoption. There has been some controversy over the exploitation by birthmothers of adoptive parents who are desperate for a child. Some birthmothers seem more willing to give their children to the highest bidder in terms of money and "perks" than to do what might be best for the child. These women need to look at their true feelings about having to give up their babies and to stop acting out their anger and frustration by making the adoptive parents "pay" for "taking away" their babies.

There needs to be a great deal more *honest* (unbiased and impartial) counseling for both biological and adoptive parents as to what all of this manipulation of parents means for the baby and for them. Perhaps counseling should be legislated, because people in the "baby business" are not going to do it for obvious reasons: Providing honest information and counseling to the birthmother about the pain of her loss, and to adoptive parents about the special problems of being an adoptive family, is a conflict of interest for people making money in adoption.

Time for a New Approach

Because of the profit motive involved in many independent adoptions today, which often lends itself to exorbitantly expensive adoption costs and even dishonest practices, it may be time to rethink and restructure adoption methods. State-controlled, non-profit agencies, which would be required to provide adequate pre- and post-adoption counseling for the birth and adoptive parents, would assure an impartial setting for adoptions. In the past, babies were kept in hospitals to languish in isolation with no one to comfort or touch them, then routinely sent out to foster parents, thus providing another potential for attachment and loss. Provisions would need to be made for the education of agency personnel concerning the primal wound and how to deal with it.

Even in agency settings the birthmother could be given some say about who would parent her baby. At the same time, for the baby's sake, she should be encouraged to maintain some post-adoption contact, whether it is painful for her or not. This contact does not have to be her physical presence, but could be in the form of letters, cards, photographs and up-dated history. The birth parents need to be real to the child, and his genetic history made available to him, but the relationship should be devoid of as much confusion as possible. The jury is still out about how best to achieve this.

In any case, it is my opinion that the birthmother needs some time alone with her baby, whether it is to welcome him into the world or to say good-bye. If both sets of parents then want to have some kind of ceremony, that's fine, so long as everyone remembers that it is for them; it is not going to diminish the trauma of loss the baby will suffer as a result of his separation from his biological mother. *It will not prevent the primal wound.*

The Need for Adoptive Parents

Even with a full understanding of the pain which she and her child will experience upon separation, some biological mothers will opt for relinquishment; there will always be children who need loving adoptive parents. Adoptive parents may need to consider that preparation for the new baby involves more than providing a nursery. Because of the understanding and special nurturing needed for traumatized babies, prospective parents can help prepare themselves for parenthood by examining very carefully their own abandonment issues, their issues concerning their infertility, their reasons for wanting to adopt, their willingness to acknowledge the differences between biological and adoptive families, their expectations for the child and the adoptive family relationship, and how it will feel for them to rear a biological stranger, a child who may be totally different from them.

Children Make a Difference

It is important for parents, whether adoptive or biological, to realize that children take a great deal of time, attention, and under-standing. It makes me very nervous when people say that they want "to have a baby." I would feel better if they would say, "I want to rear a child," understanding all which that implies. Too often in our society, people want to have children as long as these children don't interfere with their lives. Well, children are going to interfere with and change their parents' lives. If they don't, parents may not be doing a good job of parenting.

Adopted children take even more patience and understanding than biological children for all the reasons already outlined in this book. They are especially sensitive to being left in day-care centers or with rotating nannies or baby sitters, for example, because they have already experienced abandonment. (All infants and children under age three suffer from this experience, by the way. They are not ready for extended time away from mother. It is difficult for us as a society to acknowledge this, however, because we don't know what to do about it. With so many working mothers today, this dilemma has become widespread.)

Before a couple makes the decision to share their lives with a child, whether biological or adopted, they should ask themselves if they are willing to put the child's welfare first, his emotional, psychological, physical, and spiritual welfare, not just his material welfare. If not, then perhaps they should question their motives for wanting a child. Children come into the world as tiny, helpless, totally dependent beings. We owe it to them to do what is in their best interest.

CHAPTER 10

The New Family

In establishing a new adoptive family, it is necessary to distinguish between the process for a newborn and that for an older child. In this chapter I will make recommendations to adoptive parents who are adopting newborns. Many of these suggestions will be relevant to any adoptive relationship, but some modifications are recommended for families adopting older children. These will be discussed in the next chapter.

Bringing Baby Home

Once the baby is in his new home, it is important for the adoptive parents to follow some guidelines to help the attachment and bonding processes. Eye contact is very important. A baby should always be held while being fed, with eye contact being maintained throughout. Skin to skin contact is also important between infant and mother, so that he can begin to feel more secure with the new scent, energy, and heartbeat in a calm, loving atmosphere. Touch is a basic need of all babies. At this early phase, infants learn about people and objects through sensory perception and intuition.

For babies who do not respond to cuddling, it is essential to find ways to touch them in a loving way that is nonthreatening. There are people who specialize in baby massage, and I would recommend that parents seek one out in order to learn some techniques which will allow the baby to accept touch without feeling threatened. Certain games which foster touch can be another means of doing this.

Parents should not mistake a child's reluctance to accept cuddling for a lack of a need for closeness and touching or a rejection of them. The child needs touch, but may not trust it. It is up to the parents to devise ways to make sure that there is no deficit in this area. Some children provoke spankings to fulfill the requirement for touch. If a child seems calmer after a spanking, it is probably because he managed to get his quota of touching without becoming vulnerable, not because he feels repentant. Because this kind of touching sets up an equation where touch is also punishment for negative behavior, this form of touching sets a bad precedent. A child who does not respond positively to cuddling is only trying to defend himself against further wounding. It has nothing to do with the parents personally. They need to accept this, remain sensitive to their child's messages, and find ways which are nonthreatening to give affection.

How to Handle Loss

Parents of babies and toddlers adopted at birth or later will want to be alert to unexplained sadness or crying, which might be expressions of the child's loss of the biological mother. Remember that some psychologists believe that children up to the age of two or three can remember their birth, relinquishment, and adoption. It would be important to empathize with the loss and to talk about it—put it into words for him. If the child cries and refuses to let the adoptive mother comfort him, perhaps he is remembering his first mother and would benefit from someone saying so. "You must miss her, sweetheart," or some understanding phrase would do. The adoptive mother is certainly the nurturing mother, but she will never take the place of the birthmother, and, even if she feels threatened by this, she needs to let the child know that she understands his loss.

Also important would be noticing the adoptee's reactions to present loss (the death of a pet or of someone to whom he felt close, moving to a new community, leaving friends, etc.). Does he acknowledge the loss or does he act as if it doesn't matter? (Translation: It would be too overwhelming to do so.) Not only might the child be experiencing the immediate loss, but his first loss as well.

It is helpful to remember that the vague loss felt by the adoptee is not confined to the loss of the mother, but also to the loss of part of himself, or his Self. It is reported to feel something like phantom-limb pain or death. One of the things that adult adoptees tell me, when they get to the point where they can put words to very early feelings, is that they felt as if they had died—that the person they are is not the same person who was born to their first mother. Death and losing the mother are often confused by the child. Usually, in his confusion, the child feels as if losing the mother/death of the soul is his own fault.

The biological mother, whether overtly acknowledged or not, is a very real part of the adoptee's emotional life. This is one reason that it is important he be allowed to talk about her. Parents should communicate in a sensitive manner any information they have about the birthmother or birthfather when the child asks about them. Talking freely about them helps to keep the fantasies at bay and promotes an atmosphere of honesty and trust between the adoptee and his adoptive parents. In any case, it is my opinion that the child should be told about his adoption at an early age, even before he understands the words. There needs to be an openness about it, because he already knows about it. *He was there.* Just because he will not be able to consciously remember it, doesn't mean that it isn't affecting him.

Telling About Adoption

While it is important to talk about adoption from an early age, it is equally important to remember that, intellectually, adoption is an adult, complex concept, which the child will not understand for some time. One should start with birth and go from the simple to the complex. It is crucial not to lie, and to bring the ideas naturally into the conversation. It goes without saying that the parents should be the ones to tell and that they should at the same time convey love, honesty, and permanency (which doesn't mean that the child will be able to accept it that way). He should be free to discuss adoption all his life, because it is a lifelong process.

The goals are both *telling* and *understanding*, and both must be completed. Some of the questions which might come up are the nature of adoptive family relationships, the nature of the adoption process, the parents' motives for adopting, and the birth parents' reasons for relinquishing. Sometimes adoptees appear to be disinterested in their adoption. This is a defense. They are *very* interested. Parents need not be put off by any defensive attitudes, but should proceed in a sensitive, gentle manner.

There is a *sequence of telling*, which I first heard at a workshop in Berkeley, California in 1985, sponsored by Parenting Resources (of Tustin, California) and the Post Adoption Center for Education and Research (PACER) in the San Francisco Bay Area. It may act as a guide for parents:

- *First three years*: The explanations should be kept simple. The child may believe that everyone is adopted.

- *Kindergarten*: The child knows that he did not grow in the adoptive mother's womb. Differences between him and his parents are all right (transracial, etc.). The child may want to see where he came from (agency or hospital). He may need answers to others' questions: "Where did you get that red hair?" Answer: "From my family."

- *Ages eight through eleven*: The concept of adoption broadens. The child has a unique status. He may become more overtly frightened about losing his family and needs to have his permanency reaffirmed. This is best done by action, not words; and there should certainly *never* be any threats of abandonment, such as "If you can't do better in school, we will send you to boarding school," or "We can't tolerate that behavior and may have to put you in a treatment center." Any threats to abandon, which these are, so far as the child is concerned, only serve to raise the anxiety level, causing any acting-out behavior to become more blatant and unacceptable. The child may have some fantasies about his birth family and may ask about it. He needs as much honest information as is available. Let him be the one to ask what kind of information he wants, because that is the information he is ready to hear.

- *Teens*: The adolescent will be able to understand the law (that his birth family was signed away), and about sex and relationships. He will have more understanding about his parents' reasons for choosing to adopt. There should be openness in discussing infertility.

The adolescent adoptee will need more information about his biological family as it becomes more and more apparent that he has no long-term history with the people with whom he is living. Clues to his own identity will be important to him, and it may be that he will begin to think about searching during this stage of development.

In transracial adoptions, the adoptee will need information about his heritage and should have access to appropriate role models. (This may come up before adolescence, but because of the conflicts about identity, it becomes more acute during this stage.) Parents should examine their own prejudices. It should never be assumed that parents who adopt minority children have no prejudices. Treating a black child who is growing up in a predominantly white community as if he were white is a kind of racism, because it denies the child the right to be who he is.

Remember that biracial children, especially black/white, frequently consider themselves and are considered by our society to be black. They will often identify more with the black culture than with the white culture and need the opportunity to do that. White couples who have no black friends should think twice about adopting a black or biracial child.

- *At all ages*: Parents must tell the truth about adoption and deal with reality.

Acknowledgment of Differences

Part of this reality is acknowledging the differences between an adoptive and a biological family. It is important to find a balance between denying the differences and insisting on the differences. Someone has come up with a curve which might serve as a guideline for parents listing five categories of differences: the insistence of differences, the assumption of differences, the acknowledgment of differences, the rejection of differences, and the denial of differences, with acknowledgment being the ideal. Listed below are some criteria of each:

- *Insistence*: All problems are blamed on adoption. There is a great deal of emphasis between biological and adopted children: the "bad seed."

- *Assumption*: Parents want gratitude. They bring up adoption negatively and unnecessarily.

- *Acknowledgment*: Adoption is seen as *one* of the factors in family problems. Family members have special sensitivities about adoption.

- *Rejection*: Parents admit, "Yes, there is a difference, but . . . " (want to forget it). They forget that the child feels the difference and needs permission to voice his feelings.

- *Denial*: Have not told child of adoption. There is a big secret in the family.

Children's Resistance to Talking about Adoption

Resistance to talking about adoption does not always come from the adoptive parents. Just as it is often difficult for adolescents to discuss sex with their parents, it is also difficult for adoptees to talk with their parents about adoption. There is a myth that the failure to talk about these sensitive subjects is the fault of the parents. While it is true that there is sometimes resistance on the part of parents to discuss these topics, sometimes the resistance comes from the child. This needs to be acknowledged.

It can sometimes be difficult for parents to locate the fine line between *allowing* children to talk about adoption and *insisting* that they do. Parents have told me that they have opened up the conversation or tried to elaborate upon something which their son or daughter has said, only to be faced with silence. They say that it is their children who often do not want to talk about adoption. In this case, it is important to be sensitive to the child's wishes, but at the same time to try to discover what aspect of talking about adoption bothers him. Children, even those whose parents seem to be open about it, often think that they are going to hurt their parents' feelings if they discuss how they are really feeling. Other children are in denial themselves about the fact that they are adopted, because it brings up the "before I was wanted by you, I was unwanted by somebody else" feeling. Parents need to be open, patient, and sensitive.

Games and Play Time

Sometimes it is helpful to play fantasy games. Find out what the child's monsters are. Children will often communicate their feelings if they can do so under the guise of a game. Puppets are especially effective for this purpose. The "Ungame" (a board game) is a good game about feelings, so long as all the participants are honest in the way they play. (In other words, the parents have to be honest about their feelings, too.) *Feelings should never be criticized or judged.*

124

Having a sandbox with different kinds of figures, animals, edifices, vegetation, and so forth can be an excellent medium in which a child can work through some of his problems, as many child therapists know. Observing the child at play can often give clues to his anxieties, although, as Marion Barnes has said, most parents do not have the necessary understanding of the ego and the mechanisms of defense to help their children work through these anxieties. A therapist, trained in adoption issues, can help the parents interpret what is going on and give advice as to how best support the child as he works through his feelings.

A child at play knows what he needs to do and will do it if left to his own devices. Parents should not direct a child's play or become concerned that he is not playing with "educational" toys. All play is educational in the sense that it is a means whereby a child can work through his feelings. I would recommend that all parents read an article by Bruno Bettelheim entitled "The Importance of Play," which appeared in the March 1987 edition of *The Atlantic Monthly*. It is an excellent article by a man who understood children very well. Too much organization of a child's time can inhibit this very important work. (This is also true of adolescents, who need some "alone time.")

Art, Poetry, Music, and Dance

Many adopted children, perhaps especially those who are more withdrawn in other ways, are very creative. The products of their creativity can often contain clues to their true feelings. If it is not intrusive, it can be helpful to observe an adoptee's art work, stories, poems and other creative endeavors. A parent has to be able to understand the symbolism involved, because the child is seldom aware of what he is "saying." This can provide valuable clues as to what is going on inside the child, because art and poetry often come from the unconscious. It is important that the parents be accepting and understanding about whatever it is that they discover. If they feel rejected or angry because they see a picture of a child killing his parents, they would do well to try to understand their own feelings, and not criticize the child. He may only be trying to work out his feelings of having been "killed," or he may have some fantasies about the adoptive parents having stolen him from his birth family (which is preferable, in his mind, to thinking that his mother give him away).

Music can offer children a means by which they can express feelings or moods. Composing their own music or interpreting other people's compositions afford a child a wide range of expression. Parents can observe (or hear) if a child composes or prefers to play or sing compositions in major or minor keys, fast or slow tempos, and so forth. Again, no comment is called for, although an acknowledgment of the mood of the piece, such as "That song makes me feel sad; is that how it makes you feel?" may make the child more aware of his own feelings.

Dance or movement is another means by which parents can get to know the inner lives of their children. Children love to dance, and the ways in which they move their bodies are often metaphors for how they feel. For instance, I have observed adopted children vehemently throwing themselves during dancing or playing activities. (They also throw things.) When one works with the meaning behind this form of expression, one often discovers that the child is acting out, over and over again, the feelings of having been thrown away. I am grateful to Suzi Biederman, a dance and movement therapist from New York, for demonstrating how she helped one little boy work through this trauma to the point of being able to have compassion for that little baby inside himself.

The parents should not question the child about what he is doing, or try to correct his fantasies. He is trying to work that out for himself. Parents who experience difficulty with the child's feelings, as symbolized in his creative endeavors, need to seek therapy or a support group to work out *their own* feelings of rejection or betrayal. They, too, have a right to their feelings, but there is often more to these feelings than what is going on in the immediate situation, and they may want to explore this.

One can gain a better understanding of a child by observing his means of creative expression. The child must be allowed to express himself freely, without criticism. If he feels criticized for his endeavors, he will stop doing this very important work (or stop leaving it where they can find it). Parents should look upon his work—a record of his pain and an effort toward wholeness—with openness, compassion, and understanding.

Separation Anxiety

One of the themes which comes up for adoptees in their play and artistic endeavors is that of being lost, forgotten, or neglected. Children who have already experienced the loss of their birthmother will find it difficult to be separated from their adoptive mothers. Day care or school is often a source of apprehension for adoptees, because it means being separated from mother. This is often exacerbated because of the difficulty many adoptees have with the academic process. If psychosomatic illness has not been evident until now, it may begin at this time. Stomach aches, often with accompanying diarrhea, can be brought on by any new situation. At such times it is important to remember that the symptoms are real, even though the cause may be psychological rather than organic.

It might be helpful to talk to the child, to say something like, "Something's bothering you, isn't it, Susan? Can you tell me about it or draw me a picture about it?" Even if the child can't immediately respond, an acknowledgment of her pain in a gentle tone of voice can begin to alleviate some of the tension and leave the door open for more communication in the future.

Stuttering and skin disorders are more difficult to address without professional help. It should be noted that parents should not assume that the child is suffering from a psychosomatic problem. *Physical symptoms need to be checked out by a physician.*

With or without accompanying physical symptoms, a child, when separated from his adoptive mother for the first time, is very likely to experience a great deal of anxiety. On both a physical and an emotional level he will be reminded (although most likely unconsciously) of that first separation. It is very important that adoptive parents avoid being late in picking up their children after school or other activities, and to write them often when they are away at camp. This is not treating them like babies; it is an attempt to lower the anxiety level of children for whom separation is a tremendously frightening experience because of their "memory" of that first devastating loss. Over and over again they need to be assured that someone understands this loss and the ease with which the fear of its happening again can be triggered.

The Meaning of Discipline

What about discipline? Even though we know that an adopted child is in a great deal of pain, he still needs to have rules for behavior in order to take his place in the family and in society. It is important to teach a child about limits and boundaries for his own well-being. This is necessary to his relationship with his parents as well as to future relationships. It is also a very important source of the child's sense. of security. Adopted children love routine and often act out when routine is interrupted, even if they look forward to new activities. Every new experience again raises the anxiety level.

One of the diifficulties in disciplining an adopted child is in knowing what is actually going on. Sometimes a behavior does not seem to have much to do with the stimulus preceding it. Parents should watch for exaggerated behavioral responses to stimuli. For instance, an adopted child has low frustration tolerance and will often kick, scream, or cry when unable to do a task easily. Ask yourself if his behavior is appropriate to the situation, or is it out of proportion to what is currently going on? (This is a good question to apply to ourselves as well as our children!) If the behavior seems out of proportion to the situation, it may be a reaction to an "old" feeling, which was triggered by a recent event. Allow the child to calm down, and then talk about what he felt was wrong. (Trying to talk while the child is in an agitated state will only result in the parent and child getting into an argument, with each becoming defensive and more and more angry.) Let him know that you realize he was very upset and you are interested in what it was that upset him.

It is not easy to get at the real stimulus (which button was pushed), because the child is usually unaware of it himself. He may be absolutely sure that his behavior was justified. (Remember that because of their early victimization and manipulation, adoptees sometimes feel persecuted by the least thing and will lash out at the parents for the confusion and chaos they feel inside.) What the parents need to watch for is their own responses to their child's behavior. (What button of *their own* unresolved conflicts did he push?) Is their wish to punish a result of their own feelings of rejection? These feelings might be normal and understandable, but they should not be acted upon. It is amazing that parents often expect a level of restraint from their children which they are not capable of demonstrating themselves. When parents react from their own "inner child," they cannot effectively parent. They should do this inner child work in their own therapy. In their relationships with their children, they should set an example of self control and should demonstrate understanding and fairness toward their children. This is not easy to accomplish, especially in the case of extreme testing-out behavior, but it is a goal to strive for.

After trying to be as careful and aware as possible about what might be going on, the parents then have to teach the child that, regardless of his reasons, his behavior has consequences. The key word here is *teach*. *To discipline means to teach*, not to punish. The method of disciplining should be appropriate to the behavior, but not punitive. This can be very difficult to adhere to with acting-out children, because they push and push until parents are often at their wit's end and will do almost anything to stop the behavior. This only serves to reinforce the child's vision of himself as a "bad" person, which then serves as a stimulus for even more intolerable behavior, with both parent and child feeling inadequate and rejected.

Younger children sometimes just need some time to "cool off." The presence of the mother at times when the child seems out of control will create even more tension and less control. Sending a child to his room *with the door open* might help, especially if there is a rocking horse, Wonder horse, or rocking chair in the room. I recommend leaving the door open so the child will not feel isolated and abandoned. Any rocking motion is soothing and often calms a child down quickly.

After the child has calmed down, follow through with a talk. It is important to first affirm the child's feelings of helplessness and being out of control, then proceed to ascertain what was going on. Recognizing and acknowledging an adoptee's feelings is prerequisite to any further process with him. He is confused and scared of his own feelings and needs to be assured that these feelings are legitimate, but that his behavior was unacceptable.

For parents of children who find it difficult to accept either love or discipline, I would recommend a book called *The One-Minute Scolding* or *Who's the Boss* by Gerald Nelson. It describes an effective method of conveying both love and discipline to a child, without parent and child ending up in frustration and anger. Because Nelson's method takes time to learn effectively, and because children often respond negatively at first, many parents give up on this method before they perfect it or before the child begins to respond in a positive way. It is important to remember, especially with children who are afraid to allow much affection, that their overt response is not necessarily what is going on inside. Keep at it. Dr. Nelson's psychological reasoning is sound, especially as it pertains to the adopted child.

Dr. Nelson's ideas are also valuable for the compliant, acquiescent child who is afraid to express his own feelings of anger for fear of being abandoned. Observing that his parents can be angry at him and still love him might begin to allow him to express his own anger about what happened to him. The withdrawn, compliant child is very deceptive. Because he doesn't cause much trouble, he therefore seems untroubled. Although he often seems affectionate, it might be a good idea to notice how willing he is to express other feelings to ascertain how real the feelings of affection actually are. Are they truly expressions of a deep, secure love, or are they an anxious response to the fear of a further abandonment? Parents often mistake clinginess for affection. Children who feel secure in their parents' love can more easily risk expressing negative feelings as well as positive feelings. No matter what the temperament of the child, whether acting out or compliant, parents should act toward him in a consistent, firm, and loving manner.

Limits During Adolescence

Being consistent, firm, and loving becomes more and more difficult as the child approaches adolescence. The testing-out child becomes even more out of control at the very time that he wants and needs more freedom. It is also at this time that some compliant children begin to act out more, as they come face to face with their identity crisis.

Parents should be understanding, but must set definite limits for behavior. At the age when peer pressure is at its peak, the pressure to experiment with drugs, alcohol, and sex becomes overwhelming. Compounded by the feeling held by many adoptees that they belong with the "losers and stoners" of life, the problems become magnified. The teenager has to be assured over and over again that his parents love him, but that love includes discipline, and discipline means limits. He needs to know that they will listen to his requests, but will stick to their convictions no matter what other parents are doing.

An example of the need to be fair and stick to convictions can be seen in the experience of a young woman named Janice. In speaking about her confusion growing up in a family where she was receiving many mixed messages, Janice said, "My parents actually had good values and a sense of fairness, but they tended not to trust their own judgment.

They often allowed me to do something which they didn't approve of simply because my friends' parents allowed them to do it. This became clear one day when I heard Mom talking to Gretchen's mom. All of a sudden I realized that my parents' moral and ethical values could be challenged with one simple telephone conversation." Instead of feeling good about this, she ended up feeling confused and unsafe.

In setting limits for their children, parents need to be fair and to take into consideration what is appropriate for teenagers at this time and place in history. Parental expectations about dress, hairstyles, language, or behavior should take into consideration the importance of the adolescent need for acceptance by peers. Rigid standards by parents, which fail to take this into account, will only invite rebellion and serve to make the child feel justified in breaking the rules. When a teenager breaks a rule about one of these less important issues, it then becomes easier to break the rules about more dangerous things, such as drugs and alcohol. "Don't sweat the small stuff" is a good rule for parents. If parents are fair, the child will appreciate their being strong and caring, even as he rails and pushes against the boundaries which they have set. (Don't expect gratitude, though, for at least another twenty years.)

Angela used to push furiously against the limits her parents set for her social relationships, yet she would be angered at the laxness demonstrated by many "lame parents, who don't care about their kids." Letting her parents know how she felt about these "lame parents" was her way of telling them that she appreciated their giving her a way to control what she was having difficulty controlling herself. "I could always blame my bitchy mom for not letting me do something" which she knew to be inappropriate or dangerous, but which she couldn't tell her friends that she didn't want to do.

Limit setting becomes even more conflictual when it concerns an activity the child does want to take part in. Holding the line can seem like a monumental task for parents. Intimidation is the name of the game: Parents are called names, sworn at, told they are not the real parents, and made to feel totally unfair and inadequate. Some parents find the constant struggle for power too difficult and give up. Yet one can't give up, because the stakes are too high. Parents need to be consistent, follow through with appropriate discipline, and always be willing to talk things over, listening to and acknowledging the child's feelings of frustration, hostility, and anger. Ultimately, fairness and consistency can result in the child's learning to set reasonable limits for himself and sticking to them in the face of peer pressure or other adversities.

The First Cardinal Rule for Adoptive Parents

One cardinal rule, no matter what the behavior, is to NEVER THREATEN ABANDONMENT. No matter how hard the child pushes for it, it is *not* what he wants; it *is*, however, what he expects. Though the child may bring you to your wit's end, restrain yourself from implying in any way that you will abandon him. Adoptive parents often feel inadequate and totally rejected as parents. Nothing they do seems enough. Those who turn to organizations such as Tough Love will be told that they have to tell their uncontrollable children to leave. I don't recommend this for adopted children who are still minors, except as a last resort, when all other avenues, such as counseling or searching, have been exhausted and the family living situation is absolutely intolerable for everyone concerned.

In the case of extremely outrageous or dangerous behavior, perhaps distance and time will be the only means for the adoptee to get some perspective on what has been going on. Sending the child away to a school or adolescent treatment center is a last resort, however. If it does happen, it is important that feelings of abandonment, loss, and rejection be explored. Abandonment was the initial trauma. Parents do not want a re-enactment of that trauma to be the undoing of a lifetime of commitment and love.

At some point, of course, it is appropriate for a child to leave home, and for the adoptee this very normal separation sometimes becomes problematic. As a young adult who may feel insecure in the love of his parents, the adoptee will find it frightening to leave home. For him a separation in any relationship often seems traumatic. Even some young adults who have spent their entire adolescence threatening to leave find it difficult to actually do so. This problem becomes compounded by the parents' feelings of guilt about having to push the young adult out of the nest. Because they may feel as if they are abandoning him, adoptive parents sometimes allow their adult child to stay at home long after it is appropriate for him to leave. Everything has its own season, and when it is time for a child to leave home, colluding with his own fears about doing so keeps the adoptee in a dependent position and reinforces his own feelings of inadequacy and unworthiness. Adoptive parents can acknowledge their child's fears, while at the same time insisting kindly and firmly that he leave and exercise his own autonomy.

Sometimes it is the mother, rather than the child, who has difficulty with the child's becoming independent and leaving home. Her own need to be needed or her emotional dependence on him takes precedence over his need for autonomy. She must look into her own issues of separation, loss, and self-esteem. The child needs his parents' permission to leave. He needs to know that they are there to help him if appropriate and possible, but that he should, at a certain time in his life, leave the nest. He needs his parents' reassurance that leaving home is appropriate and healthy and not a rejection of him. His readiness to leave the nest is a celebration of his coming of age and a vote of confidence by his parents in his ability to assume the responsibilities of adulthood.

Five Cardinal Rules

Here is a summary list of the *Five Cardinal Rules for Adoptive Parents*. They are not always easy to follow, but they are, in my opinion, essential to the well-being of the adopted child.

FIVE CARDINAL RULES FOR ADOPTIVE PARENTS

- *NEVER THREATEN ABANDONMENT.* It is what the child expects, but no matter how hard he pushes for it, it is *not* what he wants. In the short term, threatening abandonment seems like an effective behavior modifier, but in the long term, it only raises anxiety and fosters more acting out.

- *ACKNOWLEDGE YOUR CHILD'S FEELINGS.* Never say to your child, "You shouldn't feel that way." Everyone has a right to his feelings. Feelings come from the unconscious. A person doesn't have to act on his feelings, and should take responsibility for his behavior, but feelings are what they are. They mean something and should be acknowledged and respected.

- *ALLOW YOUR CHILD TO BE HIMSELF* as fully as he is able. Withdraw expectations which are alien to his personality, proclivities, and talents and value his uniqueness.

- *Adoptive mothers: DO NOT TRY TO TAKE THE PLACE OF THE BIRTHMOTHER.* You both are your child's *real* mother; she the real biological mother, and you the real nurturing mother. The child can love you both, just as you can love more than one child.

- *As difficult as it is to acknowledge, YOU CANNOT TAKE AWAY YOUR CHILD'S PAIN.* He must work it through for himself. What you can do is acknowledge his feelings and provide the means by which he *can* work through his pain.

CHAPTER 11

Adopting Older Children

Although the issues for adoptees are the same regardless of at what age they are relinquished and adopted, there are some things to consider when adopting older children. For instance, problems arise from the numerous attachments and separations which occur when children are shuttled from one foster home to another. In addition to attachment problems, adoptive parents of older children may face abuse inflicted either by members of their family of origin or by their foster family or both. These traumas place a great deal of responsibility upon the adoptive parents for understanding, compassion, and restraint in dealing with difficult behavior.

One Year of Love. . . .

Parents who adopt older children are often told such things as "one year of love for each year of abuse" and are led to believe that if they can just love enough, these children will be fine. Of course, they never can, because the children don't trust anyone or anything. Why should they? Although these children have essentially the same issues as those children adopted at birth, the problems have been exacerbated by repeated disappointments and failed attachments. They are not going to be foolish enough to trust this relationship.

Adoptive parents of abused children should be told by the social workers just how difficult their job is going to be. They have to be extremely understanding, strong, and resilient. People who adopt older children are often people who already have children, but who feel as if they want to help an unwanted child. The child often completely disrupts the family and disappoints the parents, who had some fantasy about him and their ability to help him. And they certainly can help him, but they have to pay attention to his signals.

The Issue of Touch

I mentioned earlier that touch is very important to any child (or even adult). For an adoptee who was adopted as a child, rather than as an infant, however, touch can be traumatic. Some of these children have been physically and/or sexually abused, and touch represents abuse. Telling the child that he doesn't have to worry about being abused in his present family does not help. "I won't hurt you; I just want to love you," are words many abusers use to seduce the child. Parents of these children should take their cues from the child and proceed very slowly. The child needs to protect himself against further abuse and loss.

Fear of Connection

It is, in fact, a good idea to take all things slowly with older adoptees. There may have been several attachments and separations in the life of the child, which makes each subsequent attachment more suspect. Wariness and suspicion will be evident in most cases, even as one can detect a real wish on the part of the child to be able to trust that *this* will be a family with whom the adoptee can connect for good. The wish does not translate into trust. No matter how much the parents try to convince the child that they are not going to abandon him, he will expect it to happen. It is his experience. It is going to be very difficult for him to even begin to trust. Parents *must* understand this and not personalize the child's rejections of their efforts. The child is simply defending himself against being hurt again. Rejection is a hair-trigger for adoptees, especially those who have suffered several broken attachments, so adoptive parents should not expect miracles. They need to stay calm, even if their child is not. These kids can be *very* provocative and get the parents hooked into their system.

Many parents of older adopted children, even if they don't want to admit it, have some kind of missionary zeal involved in these adoptions and are surprised, disappointed, and angry when the child is not grateful for their good intentions. Not only are many of these children not grateful, but they are angry, suspicious, and hostile. Such feelings are normal for children who have been in foster care, especially those who have been abused. It doesn't matter that the adoptive parents have no intention of abusing him. He doesn't know that. He was probably taken out of an abusive biological home and put into the foster-care system, which also may have been abusive. He has absolutely no reason to trust his new situation and won't for a long, long time, if ever.

To these parents, I want to say this: If the child treats you as if you were abusers or potential abusers, let him know that you understand his fears that he cannot yet trust you. Tell him to take his time and to let you know if you are doing anything which seems threatening to him. He needs to feel as if he has some kind of control over what happens to him. It is essential that abused children, especially if they were sexually abused, get professional help. Both you and the child need and deserve this help.

Meanwhile, don't try to defend yourselves against any accusations he may make against you. Just say that you understand why he might feel the way he does and that you know he will just have to find out for himself if his feelings are valid *for you.* Remember that adoptees project onto the adoptive parents much of what has happened to them before and many of the feelings that they themselves have inside. *Arguing with them about this does absolutely no good; acknowledging the feelings does.*

Being Empathic

An adoptee who has been in several foster homes is not going to accept this new family as his family right away. He has been disappointed too many times before. The new family should practice a little at a time to be a family. Do things that are fun, exciting, and silly, then allow time for the child to integrate the experiences. Have empathy with his past without being intrusive, listen without judgment, validate feelings, and try to understand his helplessness and sorrow. He will probably not be able to communicate his feelings overtly, and parents should try to become acquainted with his symbolic expressions of love and loss. Remember that he has suffered multiple losses and is grieving. He wants to be able to trust your love, but he can't. Be patient!!

One of the things you may notice as parents of older adopted children is that the child may regress to a younger age at first and periodically thereafter. This is normal. He has to grow up in his experience with you. He may even wet the bed, which may be a combination of regression and anxiety. Don't punish him. Just let him know that it must be tough to be in yet another home and that you know that it will take some time for him to adjust. Let him act like a two-year-old, if he feels like it. Just be as understanding as you can. Understanding, patience, and acknowledgment of feelings are essential in parenting older adopted children.

If you begin to feel rejected by him, let this act as a hint as to how he must be feeling inside, although a hundred times more strongly. And no matter how much he acts out and makes you feel bad, you are the adult, you are the parents, and you *must* be the ones to remain in control of your reactions to your emotions. This is not easy, as many of you know or will find out. If you find that you cannot do so, get help. Don't try to be a martyr. If he acts out his feelings overtly, this will be the ultimate test, and you have to be ready for it. He wants security; he wants boundaries; he wants limits in order to feel safe, but he will fight you about them until you will feel like giving up. Don't! He is rebelling against your control because he feels the need to be in control; at the same time he knows that he isn't. Parents have to be strong, and above all, *fair.*

No matter how much they may rebel against it, limits are extremely important to adoptees, especially those who have been moved around a great deal. They thrive on routine and consistency. This gives them a sense of security. Often in their various homes, they have been given mixed messages, so they need to know that what one says is what one means, and the verbal message must be consistent with the body language and the facial expressions. Children are not fooled by words which do not match the unconscious expressions of whoever is communicating with them.

Difficulties in School

It would be unfair to think that kids who have been shuffled around will do well in school. They are full of anxiety, which precludes their being able to concentrate for very long. Help them to do their best, but lower your expectations. Many of these children are taking in a great deal more information than they are able to put out in the forms of tests or homework. Schools are very limited in the methods they have for assessing children's learning capacities, intellectual and/or creative functioning, or acquired knowledge. Just because your child is not functioning well in school does not mean that he or she is not intelligent and not learning.

It is important for everyone involved in the education of these children to understand that the reason these children have so much

140

trouble is experiential, not biological. Children who feel abandoned fear abandonment, and keeping this from happening again takes energy and concentration away from academic pursuits. Children who suffer from fetal alcohol syndrome may have even more difficulty than children whose birthmothers did not have substance abuse problems. However, any version of the "bad seed" or defective gene pool theory as an explanation for adopted children's academic problems is non-sensical. That whole theory is right out of the dark ages and deserves to be buried once and for all.

The expectations which many adoptive parents have for their child's academic standing may never be realized because of the child's anxiety and inability to concentrate. Putting more pressure on him will only exacerbate the problem, filling him with more anxiety. When a child's primary activity becomes protecting himself from further abandonment, it leaves little energy for concentrating on other less life-threatening activities such as school work. To get an idea of what this hypervigilance is like, watch a bird pecking in the garden. Notice how the bird is constantly lifting up its head and looking all around for signs of danger. This is what it is like for the adoptee. Even though he may not be consciously aware of what he is doing, he is constantly on the alert for signs of possible rejection—the potential for abandonment.

Many adoptees are easily distracted and do not seem to be paying attention in class. The daydreaming that many teachers complain about is an altered state of consciousness often associated with trauma victims (which these kids are). Because of concentration problems, adoptees have a great deal of trouble with finishing assignments and with testing. Many are classified as learning-disabled and suffering from attention deficit disorder (ADD). Expectations should be kept reasonable and flexible. Although all children should be encouraged to do their homework and to do their best in school, there may be times when lowering the child's anxiety level would be more important than his doing his homework. This is difficult to get across to parents who may be measuring their own worth through their child's school performance.

The Teachers' Responsibilities

Perhaps one day someone will devise a means to reach these young students through different ways of teaching and testing, so that their anxiety will not paralyze them, and their intellectual potential will be realized. Meanwhile, it would be helpful if teachers would not send these children from the room for behavioral or inattention problems. This is a form of rejection and abandonment and only serves to raise the anxiety level and to reinforce their belief in themselves as defective, bad persons.

When a child behaves inappropriately, one effective practice is to put one's hand on the child's shoulder and say something to the effect: "You seem to be having a difficult time, Johnny. Why don't you just put your head down (or get a drink of water or sit in the rocking chair—rocking chairs are great soothers of anxious children) until you feel better able to get on with your work." The simple acknowledgment of the child's feelings, rather than a criticism of his behavior, has a calming and positive effect on him. Even if he has to be isolated in the room, it is better than sending him out of the room (rejecting him). Teachers should evaluate the importance of their assignments. Is all that homework really necessary or is some (much) of it "busy work"? It is important to be honest and to give anxious children only as much work as they can handle.

Discussing the Biological Family

Adopting an older child often means that the child has some memory of his biological family. He may have been taken from them because of abuse or neglect. Talking about the biological parents becomes a sensitive issue. Although it makes no sense to such a child to say that his mother really loved him when he probably remembers the abuse, neither is it right to make disparaging remarks about any child's biological parents, no matter what the circumstances of the separation. The child needs to be able to express his anger about what happened to him, but the adoptive parents should acknowledge *his* feelings without voicing their own. We all like to be able to complain about our families, but we don't like to hear anyone else doing so.

Sometimes rather than talking about his anger, the child will act it out with the adoptive parents, especially the mother. This form of "getting the anger out" can be quite abusive to the adoptive parent, yet some of it has to be tolerated. One has to be more flexible about rules for speech and behavior when one adopts abused children because of the anger abuse engenders. Allow the child to express his anger verbally, even if this means swearing. Swearing is only words. Try not to get too defensive when the swearing is directed at you. Don't say, "Why are you yelling at me? I'm the one who took you in when your parents were abusing you." As I said before, these children did not ask for their lives to be manipulated in this way, and they have no reason to be grateful for it.

Empathize with the feelings, and try to direct the reactions to the feelings to more appropriate means of expression. Get a punching bag or a trampoline and try to get your child to use them when things are getting out of control. Sometimes verbalizing the feelings is not going to be enough. These children are enraged, not just angry. And part of their rage comes from having been taken away from their parents, no matter how abusive they were. Remember the quotation from Judith Viorst earlier in the book. In the child's eyes taking him from his parents, even from an abusive situation, may seem more abusive to him than staying with them.

Any adopting couple needs to look at their attitudes toward the birthmother (and father, if he is known) as well as toward the genetic inheritance of the child. Genes do count in determining the personality of the child, but adopted children have no better or worse genes than anyone else. What they do have is a deep and difficult-to-heal wound, which is a result of a devastating experience and which takes a great deal of patience and understanding to help heal.

The Wounded Parents

Sometimes helping their child to heal his wounds becomes difficult for the adoptive parents, because in the process of the child's communicating his pain (by acting out the chaos and anger he feels inside), the parents themselves become wounded. What often happens is that they then begin to respond to their own feelings of being rejected, inadequate, and unappreciated. They feel inadequate as parents and angry about their apparent ineffectiveness, often taking out their frustrations on the child. This sets up a circuitous pattern of rejecting behavior on the part of both the parents and the child. This all too often culminates during adolescence with the child's being kicked out of the home, placed in psychiatric treatment centers, or leaving of his own volition. Any of these scenarios leaves everyone feeling rejected and a failure.

Adoptive parents need not assume that they are ineffective parents just because the child is acting out. As was stated before, the child is usually responding to what happened before he entered the adoptive family. However, the child's early trauma should not be used as an excuse for the couple to avoid exploring what is going on in their marriage or in their relationship with the child. Effective communication between couples is one of the oft-cited deficits in a relationship, and issues brought about by the introduction of an adopted child into that relationship will often exacerbate any already established problems. Their job is a difficult one, and a good relationship between them is essential for the well-being of the marriage and the child. What they have taken on is parenting plus . . .

Healing the Adoptive Parents

As difficult as it is to do because of the demands made upon them by the adoptee, the adoptive parents would do well to take good emotional care of themselves and their nonadopted children, in addition to caring for the adoptee. It might help them to keep in mind that they can only *help* him heal; they can't take away his pain nor eliminate his past experience. He will need to work the pain through for himself.

144

Adult adoptees who are reading this book might be surprised to know that their parents need to heal, too. There are ways in which an adult adoptee can help heal the wounds of his or her parents as well as those of the siblings. The most important thing to do is first to recognize and then to withdraw any projections he may have toward his adoptive parents and to see them as they really are: people with feelings and problems of their own. He can begin by checking out, not only the true nature of the expectations his parents had for him, but how they felt about a multitude of things concerning him as he was growing up. He may find out that his perceptions were right or he might be surprised to learn that they were wrong. In any case, he will have taken the first step toward some kind of reconciliation and a new way to relate to his adoptive parents.

The parents should examine not only their expectations for their child, but those they have for themselves, as well, and find ways in which to reward themselves as good parents. Their job is a difficult one. This is especially true for the parents of children who were abused and those who act out. The mother, especially, is under tremendous pressure to prove over and over again her commitment to her child and her permanence in his life. It is difficult to imagine how outrageous the provocations and demands can get, and only an adoptive mother who has lived through it can know what it is like. It generates a great deal of pain for her, and her feelings toward her child are often confusing. She should know that her feelings are normal: She does not always have to feel love for her child. She does need support, education, and counseling. She needs to get into groups to feel less isolated. She also needs time to herself. She needs to know that she is not a failure, and that she is making a difference in her child's life.

Taking Care of the Biological Children

Sometimes parents who adopt older children already have children of their own. For those biological children, living with an adopted sibling, especially if he is an acting-out child, is often experienced as living with a handicapped child who requires 90 percent of the attention, leaving them feeling less important. They are often expected to accommodate the adopted sibling because he did not have the advantage of being born into the family.

Although not necessarily wanting to relate to their mother in the same way that the adopted sibling is relating to her, these children are sometimes jealous of the intensity of the relationship between the adopted sibling and their mother. There is frequently a concomitant feeling of guilt on the part of the biological children at not having been adopted. A great deal of overcompensation goes on to make up for this (which, in my opinion, does not work to the advantage of either the adoptee or the other children). Much of the family dynamics seems unavoidable, however, because of the need of the adopted child to be in constant control of the environment. He feels this to be a matter of life or death. (The rest of the family often feel as if it were killing them!)

A Word About Fathers

Because most adoptees have never known their fathers, the major portion of my discussion has been directed toward the child's relationship with his mothers, biological and adoptive. It was the mother to whom the child was attached and probably bonded before birth, and a mother with whom most adopted children tend to work out the trauma of the severed bond. In the case of older children, however, the father may have been a part of that child's life. The quality of that relationship will help determine the level of trust a child will subsequently have in the adoptive father. If the biological father/child relationship was an abusive one, there may be ambivalent feelings toward the adoptive father as the available target for feelings of anger, disappointment, and fear. Even if there was no abuse, feelings about having been separated from his biological family may make the adoptive father's role more immediate and more problematical than would be the case had the child been adopted at birth.

But fathers are not only important in the lives of older adoptees; they are important in the lives of all children, and I am of the opinion that when a woman considers having a child, whether biological or adopted, without the presence of a father (or male role model) in their lives, the child will be at a disadvantage. As far as the child is concerned, mothers and fathers are not interchangeable. The child needs both parents. A father has an important role in the life of his child, but it is a different role from that of the mother. And *his* real importance comes later in the child's life than that of the mother.

There comes a time in the life of every child when it is appropriate to move away from mother a bit in order to establish other emotional bonds. A father may be the best person to facilitate this. If a child doesn't move away from the mother in the safety of the relationship with the father, the child may end up enmeshed with her. The mother may then begin to use the child as the whole focus of her emotional life. This is too big a burden for any child, and a father can help make sure that this doesn't happen. He can begin, by the time the child is two years old, to spend time alone with the child away from home. A father can teach a child things which the mother cannot. He can bring to the family a different dynamic from that of the mother.

A father's influence on the lives of his children and his relationship to them will be different from those of the mother, and will have a different impact on the boys from that on the girls. Whether we like it or not, whether it is the result of hormones or environment, men and women, boys and girls are different from one another. (Anyone who doubts this should read Deborah Tannen's wonderful book *You Just Don't Understand.*) These differences are evident from a very young age and need not be seen as problematic.

A Chip Off the Old Block

In counseling individuals and families, it has become apparent to me that most children feel pressure to live up to some preconceived expectations coming more from the father than from the mother. Mothers are more apt to be seen as giving unconditional love than fathers, whose approval many people feel they have never attained. Fathers of adopted children, who have no biological connection and therefore lack similar inherited traits, must be especially careful to avoid any expectation that their children will follow in their footsteps or live out their unfulfilled dreams. (Of course, this is true of any father of any child, but more true in adoptive families.) Adopted children are already very good at living the false self, and any attempt to mold them into the father's image of what he or she should be like will only serve to bury deeper the true self and feed the fuel of accompanying conscious or unconscious rage. Fathers, therefore, can help their children tremendously by encouraging and fostering their children's own innate interests and talents, which can often be observed in the play and other activities of young children.

Father's Support for the Mother

Because the mother is still the one who does most of the nurturing in a family, she is the one who has most contact with the children. In an adoptive family, the mother often feels the most criticized, because the child most often feels that the mother was the abandoner. All the subsequent feelings of abandonment therefore must be worked out with the mother figure.

The father's support of the mother becomes very important, yet many adoptive mothers say that their husbands do not give this support. Because he is not having the same trouble with the child that she is, he is often critical of her, accusing her of provoking the confrontations which occur between her and the child. This gives the child more fuel for further insubordination and triangulates the family, with the father and child forming an alliance against the mother. If the father could begin to understand the true nature of the conflict between his wife and child and offer his support to her, the bond between the two of *them* would become stronger, which would benefit the whole family.

Adoptive Parents Do Make a Difference

Adoptive parents have a great responsibility and a unique relationship to their adopted child or children. Despite the trials and tribulations which can occur in these families, they can and do make a difference in the lives of children who might otherwise be kept in situations which are detrimental to them. They can and must help to heal the wounds of their child, but they must also help one another heal their own wounds. Their roles are often misunderstood and the expectations placed upon them overwhelming, especially those parents who take on the enormous responsibility of adopting older children. It would be helpful for them to form groups to gain support from people who have had or are having similar experiences, and to help them overcome their feelings of isolation.

Adopting any child who has experienced the trauma of separation from the biological family is a challenge, but when one adds to that the emotional scarring of children who have experienced multiple separations and traumas, the challenge often seems overwhelming. These children need an enormous amount of patience, care, and understanding, and a lowering of expectations about their own response to that love and care. Meanwhile society can help by having a more realistic attitude toward adoption in all its myriad aspects.

CHAPTER 12

Reunions as a Means of Healing the Adoption Triad

One of the ways in which society might help the healing process for adoption triad members would be to withhold judgment about those adoptees and birthmothers who are searching for one another. Their wish to search is a healthy response to their early bonding and subsequent separation experiences and does not reflect any wish to hurt anyone else. Often, however, as in the case of divorce, people think that they have to take sides, which implies that they are *for* one side and, therefore, *against* the other. This same mentality, unfortunately, is evident within the triad itself, thus hindering the very freedoms for which many triad members believe they are fighting.

I have written this book because I believe the connection between birthmother and child to be profound. Their individual yearning to re-establish their relationship may be what keeps them both in a state of limbo for so many years. Even when adoptees do not acknowledge their need to find their birthmothers, they often identify with her in some way.

Reunions as a Means of Healing the Adoption Triad

Several years ago I attended a conference on adoption where many adoptees and birthmothers related their reunion stories. One young woman stood up and in an emotional voice said that she did not see why it seemed so important for all those adoptees to go looking for their birthmothers. She had a wonderful adoptive mother. She didn't need her birthmother. In fact, she believed in adoption so much that when she gave birth at age sixteen (the same age her birthmother had been when this young woman was born), she relinquished the baby, knowing that it would be well taken care of. Her adoptive mother, who was sitting next to her, seemed like a warm, understanding woman. She said that it was perfectly all right with her if her daughter did want to search. They probably did have a very good relationship, but I don't think there was a professional in the room who didn't realize that, even though unacknowledged, that young woman was identifying with her birthmother by repeating her pattern of getting pregnant at age sixteen and relinquishing her baby. The pull to repeat the pattern is unconscious, yet very real. In addition to being a way to identify with the birthmother, it is often an attempt to condone the original relinquishment, making it legitimate and normal in the eyes of the adoptee. Perhaps a more overt acknowledgment would be preferable to having more and more babies born to mothers who can't keep them.

In addition to alleviating the need to repeat the pattern of the birthmother, finding her might also serve to relieve the anxieties felt by adoptees who doubt the permanency of their relationship to their adoptive parents. Reunions often seem to have a calming effect, so that there are no longer the urges to run away from home or engage in other self-defeating behaviors. It is as if the adoptee had been holding his breath for all those years and could begin breathing again. There is a release of tension and a renewal of life. Reunions can help all the adoptee's relationships, including that with the adoptive parents.

Whatever helps the adoptee will help the relationship with the adoptive parents. After all, in adopting a child, adoptive parents implicitly promise to do everything in their power to do what is best for their child. Searching for the birthmother is in the best interest of the adoptee. There may be anxiety connected with the search, and the outcome may not be what the adoptee anticipated. Searches are difficult for everyone concerned. All have been hurt. All are suffering. Because of this suffering, the dynamics of reunions can be unpredictable. Even if the reunion is not ideal, however, questions are answered and a sense of continuity is established for the adoptee.

The adoptee is the member of the triad with the most compelling reason to search. Birthmothers may also want to search, and many adoptees want to be found. But a birthmother should search only if she *knows* she will be willing to "hang in there" no matter what the adoptee does. *Under no circumstances should a birthmother search if there is any possibility at all that she might abandon her child again!* If she has expectations for her long-lost child as requisites for establishing a relationship with him, if she doesn't think she could stand the heartache should he "abandon" her (which some adoptees do in an unconscious attempt to let her know how it felt), then she should not search. A second abandonment is almost as devastating for the adoptee as the first one was, and it is much more conscious.

Everyone should keep in mind that no matter what the circumstances of the relinquishment, *no one* has been more manipulated than the child; he is the only one who has had absolutely *no* control over his life. He has been manipulated from the beginning, having been cut off from his birthright—his genealogical roots and his connection to his mother. Of all the members of the triad, he is the only one who was a helpless infant with *no* conscious understanding of what was happening to him, the only one who had *no* choice in the matter at all. He is the one who has to be considered before anyone else. It is up to both mothers to keep this in mind. Regardless of their feelings, they must take responsibility for their behavior and actions towards him, so that their child can begin to heal. *As he begins to heal, so will they.*

Searching—Emotionally Charged for Everyone

Despite the potential for healing which reunions represent, perhaps nothing brings to the fore everyone's feelings so much as search and reunion experiences. The fear of a second abandonment is ever-present in the minds of each and every adoptee who contemplates searching. The fear of being rejected by her child is forefront in the minds of birthmothers who begin to search. After all, she thinks, it is she who gave him up; why would he want her now? And the fear of losing her child to the biological mother is experienced by many adoptive mothers. Even though the reality may be much less threatening than the fear itself, these fears must not be taken lightly. Fear can immobilize one contemplating search, often prolonging the period between the initial idea of undertaking search and the actual search itself. Moreover, any attempt to reveal the profundity of the biological connection causes fear to be projected out into society, where someone ends up being labeled the "bad guy." The anger and frustration, which are triggered by many aspects of the adoption process, need an outlet, an external target. Unfortunately for everyone concerned, that target is often some member of the triad itself.

The "Bad Guy" Syndrome: The Adoptee as "Bad Guy"

Early in the search and reunion movement, the adoptee was labeled, most often by society, as the "bad guy." He was seen as ungrateful, unstable, and perhaps even pathological if he voiced an interest in finding his biological parents. After all, he grew up in a nice home, usually with "good enough" parents (to borrow Winnicott's term), so to go out looking for someone whom he "never knew" was seen as abnormal. Many adoptees had to find socially accepted reasons for searching, such as a need for medical history, in order to justify an inherent urge to find their roots and their connection with the lost mother.

Yet searching is a critical means by which to heal the primal wound and calm the anxiety which manifests itself in a variety of self-limiting or self-destructive behaviors. Searching for that biological past is actually a healthy, if somewhat terrifying, thing to do, and those who search should be seen as having a kind of strength and courage which is to be envied, not vilified. Although many people now acknowledge the validity of searching, there are still those in our society who feel that searching adoptees are ungrateful and uncaring about their adoptive parents' feelings. There is often a failure to realize that the adoptive parents' feelings pale in comparison to the painful feelings experienced by their child due to that early separation. If anyone should be grateful for adoption, it is the adoptive parents. If they are having problems with the idea of their child's searching, they need to look into their own issues of "ownership" or possession of their children, their own insecurities, and their need to still be in control of their adult children's lives.

Our legislative bodies continually assert the adoptive parents' right of possession, as many adoptees who begin to search have discovered. As one adoptee told me, "I am fifty years old and I still have to have my adoptive parents' permission to gain access to court records about my life." Or, as B. J. Lifton said, "An adopted child can never grow up. Who has ever heard of an adopted adult?" Not the courts. Not our society.

So, in addition to the fear of another abandonment or some kind of rejection by the birthmother, the adoptee has to weather the ridicule of a society which doesn't understand the tremendous and *healthy* urge to heal the wound of that original separation. It is true that reunions are often difficult and can cause further pain, but anyone who has been manipulated the way adoptees have has a right to search. Difficulties are often a result of misunderstandings about the process of the reunion relationship itself. The next chapter will explore a better understanding of that process, which is necessary to successful reunions and the potential for healing which they represent.

The Birthmother as "Bad Guy"

As more and more adoptees undertook a search, the stigma of abnormality began to wear off, and the "bad guy" label became less and less applicable. But as birthmothers, too, began to search, the "bad guy" label began to be applied to her. After all, here was the terrible abandoning mother, looking for a child she had decided that she could not keep. She had made her choice and should stick with it. What right did she have to change her mind after all that time? What right did she have to intrude into the happy lives of the adoptive family and cause turmoil? What right did she have to challenge society's ideas about what constitutes a family? the meaning of motherhood? the power of the environment to mold personalities? the right of society to manipulate lives? Birthmothers made a wonderful target for the "bad guy" label, and in some cases they bought into it themselves.

Many birthmothers *have* been afraid to intrude into the lives of their children's adoptive families. They know that many adoptive parents feel threatened by the very idea of their coming back into their children's lives. Yet they have no intention of trying to replace the adoptive parents as the parents, and most wait until the adoptee is no longer a child before beginning the search. Even so, the general public still finds it difficult to accept that these biological mothers and their adult children have a right to find one another. That adoptive parents may find search threatening may be understandable, but that society seems so bent on being judgmental about it is puzzling. A better understanding of her predicament may help society suspend judgment and, instead, look upon the birthmother with compassion.

Understanding the Birthmother

The pain and dilemma for the birthmother should not be overlooked, as we view the trauma from the point of view of the adoptee. Very often the choice of relinquishment is forced upon her. One hears birthmothers using such terms as "surrender," when referring to relinquishment. (One can almost picture a gun being pointed at her head!) In most cases, the mother bonds with the child in utero and has a covert yearning to keep him. Yet in the eyes of society, she is perceived as the one who broke the rules. She had sex and got caught. She is punished for this by being cut off from others, with no access to education or preparation for her role. When she has the baby, she is put in a double bind: She is discouraged from having any contact with it, then considered unfeeling and abandoning as a result of doing what she is told.

She is often denied access to adequate counseling and feels pressured and even coerced into giving up her child. She is not given the opportunity to feel self-worth as a mother. She is often unable to experience the child as real or to accept the relinquishment as real. She is, therefore, unable to grieve. Because of her part in the separation from the child and the fact that the child is still alive, she is allowed no rituals which might help her to accept and mourn her loss. During their lifetimes, many birthmothers will experience issues concerning family, sexuality, career, attachment, intimacy, and commitment. Most of these women are in some stage of unresolved grief, but are unaware of it or ambivalent about it. (Therapists to whom these women go for help need to be aware of this.)

Although a birthmother may be dealing with inconsolable pain and grief, she cannot undo what has happened, and must work through the grief and learn to accept her history. Often the reunion will bring this to the fore by her realization, upon the meeting, that her child is no longer a baby (something she of course knew in her head, if not in her heart) and that those lost years can never be recovered. She may need individual or group therapy to help her in this process. Breaking the silence of what was often a secret pregnancy, whether by means of the search or some other method, means that the wounds have to be opened for everyone. This is healthy in the long run, because one of the most debilitating aspects of any person's life is secrets.

A Double Loss

In many cases the birthmother may be dealing with a double loss. Often in the case of pregnancy, because of a denial of responsibility or unresolved blame and guilt, the relationship between the birthmother and birthfather comes to an end. Both feel out of control and each blames the other. Even if the relationship does need to end, it might be beneficial if the partners could at least try to resolve the issues between them and mourn their loss together. Depending on their age and maturity, they could be of great comfort to one another.

Unfortunately, as is true in other relationships when tragedy strikes, at the very time when the partners could truly help each other, they cannot seem to be there for one another. There is often a great deal of anger involved, which is often distorted and gets displaced onto the agency, adoptive parents, or one another. This anger is often a defense against the sadness, which both feel. They must move on to sorrow. It would be helpful to seek some kind of counseling in order to acknowledge and work through their feelings, so that each could go on with their lives without the burdens of unresolved grief, anger, blame, and guilt. These unresolved feelings often paralyze the birthmother and make it impossible for her to "get on with her life." It is now recognized that many birthfathers are also in a perpetual state of unresolved grief over the loss of their children.

The Impact on the Extended Family

The impact of giving birth to a baby who is put up for adoption does not end with the birthmother or birthfather. It has an impact on all family relationships. The extended family feels the loss, grief, guilt, etc. There are often rescue fantasies by other members of the family, as well as guilt felt by the mother's parents. Often the relinquished child is a first grandchild, which creates a profound sense of loss in the birth parents' parents. If the birth of the child is kept a secret from some family members and friends, this puts an added burden upon those who know to hide their grief and remain stoic in the face of their loss. The keeping of secrets, whether within the adoptive family or the birth family, will exacerbate the feelings of anger, shame, and guilt, and delay the healing powers of the grieving process. Often the decision of the birthmother to search is the first time many members of the family will have heard of her original loss. Most, when they do learn of her pain, wish they had been told so they could have supported her during that difficult time in her life.

Problems in the Birthmother's Nuclear Family

The unresolved conflicts within the birthmother herself will affect her relationships with her future husband and children, if, indeed, she does get married and have more children. Many birthmothers fail to marry and suffer from secondary infertility. According to reliable statistics, 38 percent of them fail to conceive again. Because she "gave away" her first child, she will often think of herself as an unfit mother, either unable to have more children or unable to care for them properly. Some of those who do give birth again feel disloyal to the lost baby and find it difficult to think of themselves as good mothers. They have a secret and may be found out! It would help if society could understand the anguish experienced by these mothers and treat them with respect and compassion. A birthmother certainly needs the understanding and respect of her husband, not only in her sorrow, but in her need to search for that child.

Reconnecting as a Part of the Healing Process

In relinquishing her child, the birthmother did what she or some- one else felt that she had to do. Although her fears that her relinquished child feels abandoned are probably true, this does not mean that she must forever chastise herself for that relinquishment. It means that she has to accept what has happened and allow herself to mourn her loss, whether it is the loss of the child or the loss of those early years in his or her life. She needs to regain her sense of Self and to reframe the experience, so that her attitude toward the past can be altered and the wound begin to heal.

One of the ways she can begin to heal is to reconnect with her lost child. And many of these mothers have taken that courageous step toward reunion, because the urge to search overpowered the fear of rejection by the child, the threat this might pose to the adoptive parents, or the disapproval of our society. And it is my opinion that no matter what anyone else thinks, every adoptee, on some level, wants that mother to find him or her—wants to know that she cares. But as I said earlier, if the birthmother does choose to search, instead of waiting for her child to find her, she must be prepared to allow the adoptee to control the relationship after reunion. Many adoptees have been hurt by their birthmother's requirements for a relationship, or by her impatience with his need to process the reunion at his own pace. If she can allow him to control the process, then her search for her child in itself can be healing for him. As birthmothers do begin to search, reunite, and form an alliance with the lost child, there needs to be another "bad guy." That's where the adoptive parents come in.

Another Shift in Roles: The Adoptive Parents as "Bad Guys"

If one attends adoption conventions, where one meets many adoptees and birthmothers who have searched and found their lost relatives, there is often an undercurrent of negative feelings toward the adoptive parents. Many adoptive parents feel this, feel shunned by the members of the other two sides of the triad, and vow not to attend another convention. What the adoptive parents may be feeling is the reassignment of the role of "bad guy" to them.

Adoptive parents do have feelings about reunions, and some of them have not been very enthusiastic or cooperative about helping their children search. However, pinning labels on them and failing to take the time to understand their feelings is no more helpful than blaming the birthmother for giving up her child or the adoptee for not being grateful for having had his life manipulated. Everyone is yearning for understanding, yet triad members are often not very understanding of one another. This is unfortunate, because if we don't own and understand our own feelings, if we cannot acknowledge and

159

empathize with one another's feelings, how can we expect those outside the triad to do so?

Search and the Adoptive Mother

It is not difficult to understand why many adoptive mothers are not overjoyed by the idea that their children want to search. After years of struggle and constant turmoil in the home, after the aching agony of witnessing their children relate more easily to everyone else's mothers than to them (it's safer!), they then see their children yearning to find that magical person with whom there is some undeniable, indefinable connection. It is mysterious and scary and makes many adoptive parents wonder why they subjected themselves to so much rejection and pain for this result. The idea that the reunion may enhance their own relationship with their adopted child is an intellectual idea and has little to do with feelings (just as the *reason* for their relinquishment is an intellectual idea, which does not make adoptees *feel* better for having been relinquished, although they may understand it better.) One thing every adoptive mother knows in her heart is that her child's reuniting with her birthmother will change forever their relationship to one another. That's the unknown. That's what makes it so scary.

We are all at the mercy of powerful feelings, which only those who have experienced the same events can truly know. For instance, although I can try to imagine it, it is impossible for me to truly know what it is like to have been relinquished. Nor can I know what it feels like to have given up a child. It is possible to *understand* another's experiences, but not to *know* them. In the same way, I don't believe that a person who has not had the experience can really know how it feels to take a baby into one's life to love and care for as one's own, yet always feel as if one cannot get quite close enough to truly bond with that child. Just as the birthmother was lied to about how easy it would be to give up her baby and get on with her life, adoptive parents have been lied to about the ease with which these babies would accept them as parents. (Perhaps "lie" is too strong a word, since most of what was told both mothers had more to do with ignorance than with malice.) Nevertheless, neither the birth parents nor the adoptive parents are prepared for the impact of separation and loss.

If one adds to that the constant provocation, defiance, hostility, and aggression of those adopted children who act out their own anxiety, frustration, and rage, it becomes clear why adoptive parents, especially mothers, must have a special kind of strength in order to survive. Many, perhaps as a result of their own abandonment issues, do not, as the statistics show. They are left feeling inadequate, discounted, rejected (often actually "abandoned" themselves by their counterphobic, runaway children), and looked upon by society as not having been loving and caring enough.

It is understandable, therefore, that the adoptive mother may very well feel threatened and hurt by her child's desire to search. If we could all adhere to the altruistic idea that all people are the children of God and that no parents "own" their children, perhaps these feelings would not be so prevalent. But, at least in our Western culture, few people are so cosmic in their perceptions. Adoptive parents are no exception, unless like some of us, they have struggled through years of therapy or some kind of soul-searching with their child to the point of being spiritually and psychologically ready to "relinquish" the child herself into a different kind of relationship from that into which she came in the beginning. *This is not easy.* It goes from the realm of the personal into that of the transpersonal. Not everyone is ready to do that (including some birthmothers). In the meantime, it is important to recognize, acknowledge, and accept without judgment that the adoptive parents may be feeling rejected and threatened.

The adoptive mother must be allowed to admit that she feels threatened by the birthmother's coming back into the life of their child. She may feel something like the mother in a divorce case, where she has all the responsibility of making sure that the homework is done and the room is clean, while the father gets the fun of having the kids every other weekend and going to the zoo. Although this may not be the reality (in either divorce, where the father may want to have more say in the day to day life of the child, or adoption, where the birthmother feels that she would give anything to have done all that nurturing), it may be the way she *feels*. She has done all the work (and because of the child's having been in pain, this was very difficult work); then the birthmother waltzes into the child's life and acts as if she has a right to be there (*which she does*). And, at least during the "honeymoon" phase of the reunion, the adoptive mother feels left out, discounted, and a hindrance to the reunion process. While she has every right to her feelings about this, she does not have the right to interfere with the reunion between the biological mother and child. Their fundamental right to be together transcends any feelings she may have about it. She does not have conscious control over her feelings, but she does have control over her response to her feelings—over her actions.

This is a very important distinction—the difference between feelings and intellectual understanding. Helping their children search is one thing; being expected to like it is another. Adoptive mothers, and perhaps especially those with the most "mother instinct," on some level perceive what a strong bond there is between the adoptee and the birthmother. (Adoptive mothers with biological children *know* this.) This is felt as primal, mystical, mysterious, and a barrier to her own bonding with her adopted child. As her child begins to search for his first mother, she may, indeed, experience a pang of apprehension, a concretizing of her long-held feeling that she has never been able to replace that lost mother. She may experience this as a failure on her part. It isn't. It was an impossible goal in the first place, and she would be better off recognizing what she *did* do than regretting what she didn't, what she *couldn't*, do.

It has been my experience, in talking and working with adoptive families, that most of the parents believe that their children will search someday. Most, if they are being honest, have mixed feelings about it; yet all say that they will help their children when the time comes. Meanwhile, they are interested in the idea of trying to update information about the birth parents, believing that both the information and the search will improve their children's self-esteem and sense of Self. These, of course, are parents who are already aware of adoption issues and are helping their children work them through.

Unfortunately for both themselves and their children, there are some adoptive parents out there who still believe that the signing of those original relinquishment and adoption papers severed not only the legal rights and responsibilities of the biological parents, but the psychological, emotional, and spiritual ties between them and their children as well. This is wishful thinking, a denial of reality, which only widens the gulf between adoptive parents and their children.

The Feelings of the Birthmother toward Adoptive Parents

The adoptive mother's alienation from the reunion process becomes even greater if the birthmother criticizes her role as their child's mother and harbors resentment towards her. If the adoptee acted out, the birthmother may find out that all was not wonderful in the adoptive home. Failing to understand the impact of the original separation on the child, she may blame the adoptive parents for not being good enough parents. In addition, she may feel a great deal of resentment toward the adoptive mother for having been the one to have done all the nurturing of their child (and, if there are problems, blame her for not having done it right). Yet she may be reluctant to acknowledge these feelings, or she may feel guilty for having them. These, too, are feelings which must be owned and acknowledged *and which are completely understandable*, but they must not cloud her judgment when it comes to how she acts in her relationship with her child and his adoptive parents. In the long run, this would interfere with her relationship with him as well as with them.

Her feelings may become extreme, as with those birthmothers who feel as if the adoptive parents stole her child from her and that adoption should be abolished altogether so that pregnant women would not be coerced into giving up their babies. "If there hadn't been any prospective parents out there to take him, I wouldn't have been put in that position," she reasons. Her pain is understandable, but her reasoning is specious. The dearth of good foster homes for children whose parents are unable or unwilling to care for them belies the no adoptive parents/no adoptable children argument. And although there is often a lack of honest counseling for the birthmother and a subtle or not-so-subtle kind of coercion which still goes on in adoption proceedings, the blame for what happened to her may be misplaced.

Birthmothers must understand that it is the institution of adoption which needs to be reformed. It may not be fair to blame the unconscionable acts performed by adoption agencies or attorneys upon the prospective adoptive parents. Most of them are just following the ancient instinct to parent. It is natural to want to have children, and many adoptive parents are unaware of what is being said to the birthmothers by agencies, attorneys, or other adoption facilitators. They have been lied to as much as the birth parents have, often because of ignorance, but sometimes because of self-serving greed on the part of the adoption-for-profit facilitators. Most prospective adoptive parents have not been counseled as to the differences between biological and adoptive families, nor has it been recommended to them that they work through their infertility issues. Socio-economic status is often the number one criterion for selecting these parents, not their understanding of the issues or their psychological/emotional readiness for taking on this responsibility.

On the other hand, many pregnant women, even when receiving honest counseling, are still choosing to give up their babies. They simply ignore their pain or the potential for pain. I have spent many frustrating hours trying to get some of these young women to understand how devastating the loss of their child is going to be and how profound their pain. Some of them have complained to the prospective adoptive parents (who truly do want her to know what she is doing) that I am trying to talk her into keeping her baby. Denial is still a wonderful defense mechanism! I'll be seeing some of these women in my office twenty years from now, when the realization of their loss finally catches up with them. In many cases, it is maturity and hindsight which now makes the searching birthmother so wise. She may or may not have made a different decision those many years ago when she was so young, confused, and vulnerable. She certainly should have had better counseling—and much, much more support, understanding, and compassion.

The Adoptee—Caught in the Middle

The adoptee, meanwhile, is often caught in the middle and feels guilty for everything that is happening. He would like for his birth and adoptive mothers to like each other, just as children of divorce want the mother and father to like one another and get along. On the other hand, he *also* may have some feelings that he is not owning.

For instance, it has been my observation that some adoptees (and this largely depends upon their age) don't want to readily admit that their adoptive parents may willingly help them search. There is a part of them which feels threatened by the idea. "If my adoptive parents are so willing to help, do they really care about me? Are they trying to get rid of me?" The fear of rejection is a ubiquitous element of the adoptive relationship. The overt or covert "fight" over the adoptee, while leaving him feeling uncomfortable and guilty, at the same time makes him feel cared for and important.

It would be important for adoptees who wish to search to check out with their adoptive parents as to how they actually feel about it. Not all parents feel threatened by the idea, although most adoptees think that they would be. Some adoptive parents, whose adopted children have found their birth parents without their having been aware of the search, say that they wish that they had known, because they would have helped, and they could have saved their children from the anxiety of worrying about their feelings.

Healing the Triad

It would be my recommendation that all triad members honestly look into their own souls and assess what they are truly feeling. Those feelings are no doubt appropriate and make sense in light of the individual's history. These feelings do not have to be denied or apologized for. But if they are not owned, they will be projected upon another member of the triad. Such projections get in the way of true understanding among triad members.

If we expect people outside the adoption triad to comprehend the complexity of the adoption process, to empathize with the need for more honesty and openness in adoption laws, to try to understand the paradoxical feelings and emotions which permeate the adoption experience and how painful those experiences have been for all three sides of the triad, then we must first do all this ourselves. We cannot expect from others that which we have not been able to do ourselves. We have all heard the adage: Physician, heal thyself. Perhaps we can amend it to fit our circumstances: Triad, heal thyself.

Reunions can play an important part in that healing process. If both mothers put the well-being of the adoptee first, we will begin to see the importance of reaching out to one another in love, rather than drawing back in fear or hostility. There is no *one way* to see things. Everyone has had her own experience as well as her own perspective, which lead to her own perceptions. It is important to allow those perceptions to be challenged in order to understand the perceptions of others. Both can be right or partially right. In acknowledging this we *can* learn to love one another as we love our child. Love is not a quantitative commodity, to be rationed out or hoarded. It is possible for the triad to become an extended family, with the best interests of the adoptee as the motive for our learning to accept and love one another.

If this sounds like some kind of utopia, perhaps it is, because, despite the healing power of the reunion process, there are many inherent pitfalls, which need to be overcome as the process progresses. As I discuss some of these pitfalls and their remedies in the next chapter, I cannot over-emphasize the necessity to understand much of what goes on as paradoxical, and I appeal to both mothers for a sense of fairness and balance of which I believe most women to be capable.

CHAPTER 13

The Reunion Process

Reunions are very emotional. I have heard some birthmothers say that the reunion was perfect and they have a wonderful relationship with their child, and I have held others as they cried and said that their child doesn't care and never phones or even writes. In any case, the relationship may be quite different from that which was envisioned by the birthmother, the adoptee, or the adoptive parents. It can be just as puzzling for the birthmother as the adoptive relationship is for adoptive parents. Sometimes everything seems to be going along fine, and then the birthmother doesn't hear from her child for months on end. She is puzzled, she is hurt; and, because she is hurting, she sometimes reacts from her own hurt "child" by "abandoning" her child for the second time.

Understanding the Emotional Climate of Reunions

Many of the problems which adoptive parents faced with their adopted child will crop up between the birthmother and adoptee. This includes the adoptee's problem of compliance and the false self, which many birth parents (as well as adoptive parents) fail to recognize. More easy to identify is the experience of rejection and abandonment, which some adoptees (usually unconsciously) act out with their birth parents. Waiting for phone calls and letters from rediscovered but unresponsive children can be excruciatingly painful, as many birthmothers can verify.

It may be that in neither the case of the "perfect reunion" nor the "difficult reunion" is the adoptee acting from his true feelings, but from a protective stance. One is being the "perfect" birth child, who doesn't want to risk losing mother again; and the other is the acting-out birth child, who is testing the birthmother and wants her to know what it feels like to be abandoned. (Does this sound familiar? It will to adoptive parents.) Because in many cases the birth and adoptive parents will experience similar responses from their children, this could (and *should*) serve to help foster understanding between them as they strive to relate to their children and to each other.

I want to dwell on this idea a bit, because I believe it to be important. Both mothers may experience their child as being reluctant to accept the relationship at face value. (Remember that their first experience outside the womb was of separation and loss!) This often results in their being cautious in accepting the love and affection which the mother, whether biological or adoptive, wants to give. Distrusting the permanence of any relationship is one of the most predictable outcomes of that early separation and loss experience. The birthmother does not escape that distrust. In fact, because she was the original lost object, she is, indeed, suspect. "If she left me once, when I was a tiny baby, she can leave me again," as Gina put it. That this is not very likely does not do away with the *feeling* that it *could* happen.

A similar feeling is experienced by the birthmother, who is often afraid that if she does this or that in her new relationship with her child she will lose him again. The trauma of that loss for her sets up a recurring feeling of impending and terrifying loss. When so-called negative feelings come up in the new and tentative relationship, she is terrified that she will lose him if she doesn't make things right. Or she will get defensive and deny whatever it is that the adoptee is trying to convey to her about his feelings. He then will feel hopeless about getting her to understand him and will either conform to what he perceives she wants him to do or be, or he will distance himself from her in a self-fulfilling prophecy. In either case, she has lost an opportunity to get to know the *real person* who is her child.

What I would like to emphasize to both birth and adoptive mothers is that, even when her own inner child is being hurt in the relationship, she must *act* in the relationship as the mature adult in control of her actions. (Notice that I didn't say "in control of her feelings." She can *experience* her feelings, but *act* maturely—in the manner which I have previously described. She can then allow her hurt inner child to come out in a support group or therapy.) I can't stress enough how important it is for *someone* to be mature in these exchanges, and that someone has to be the mother (no matter how old the "child").

In any good relationship many emotions are felt and expressed, including love, hate, joy, rage, exultation, hostility, and sadness. If these feelings can be validated and accepted as true (even if they seem out of proportion in the present situation); if they can be tolerated by the birthmother, the adoptive mother, or the therapist, as the adoptee struggles to relate to them, instead of denied or defended against, a satisfactory adult relationship can emerge. When that has happened, *then* a more reciprocal exchange of expression of feelings can take place. *Then* the two adults, mother and child, can begin to relate as peers and as friends. Before a mature relationship can occur, however, a long road must be traveled. It is very important to the healing process to understand that journey.

Regression

One of the reasons that the relationship between birthmother and child is so puzzling is that upon meeting it is almost inevitable that the adoptee, no matter how old, regresses. There is a wish to go back, to do it over, to have that mother be again in that symbiotic relationship, which was severed upon relinquishment. The mother also wishes for this. She wants to be able to nurture her newborn, to hold and rock and comfort him or her, and finds it disconcerting that he or she is no longer a tiny being.

One of the things which the birthmother might notice, then, is that her child wants her to be available to him all the time, just as a newborn would. Never mind that she may have to go to work the next day, he may want to talk to her long into the night. At the beginning he may want to call her every day, at any time of the day or night . . . just to reconnect . . . just to be sure that she is there. (Therapists should be aware that this may happen in therapy, too, when one is dealing with early loss and deprivation.) And if she wants to regain his trust and re-establish the bond with him, she will allow this *for awhile.*

I say "for awhile," because I don't think that it is appropriate for either reunited birthmothers or therapists to allow this severely regressed behavior for very long. We can take our cue from other members of the animal kingdom, where one will notice that it is the mother who determines when a young bird will leave the nest or a lamb will stop suckling. She can then gradually let her "child" know that, even though she is still available, he cannot expect her to be available 24 hours a day. If she is acting like a "mother" in the relationship and making strong suggestions to him about how he should be conducting his life, he will want her to stop "mothering" him and will begin to see the advantage of not being so dependent on her availability, which will begin to feel like interference or engulfment. In both the reunion and therapeutic relationships, there will be a natural progression or "growing up process" after the initial regression. This has to be fostered by the parent figure in both cases, fostered with encouragement, sensitivity and firmness. (Watch the mother bird teaching her fledglings to fly.) That's what is happening. The birthmother has given her child back his wings and is teaching him to fly.

Sometimes the adoptee begins the reunion relationship by being somewhat receptive to the birthmother, then cuts off the relationship, leaving her without word for months at a time. As difficult as this is for her, she must accept this as part of what her child has to go through. He may be feeling overwhelmed by his emotions and need to proceed very slowly, putting time and distance between him and his new-found mother. Or he may be testing her, just as he may or may not have previously tested the adoptive parents. No matter how rejected she feels and how much she believes that her child does not want anything to do with her, *he does.* She must be patient. She must keep sending those cards and letters, calling on holidays, and generally keeping in touch. As one insightful and sensitive birthmother put it, "Our children still need to hear from us, even if they don't respond." She has to be the mature one in the relationship, no matter how much she is also hurting, no matter how much her own internal "abandoned child" is crying out.

Some birthmothers will say, "But why should I? I'm hurting, too! It sounds as if you are putting all the responsibility for the relationship on me." And she is right. If she wants to let her own inner child run rampant, to be running the show, then she can certainly do so. But if the long-term goal is a positive relationship with her child, then she needs to take on the responsibility of the relationship in its early stages. As with a newborn child, this "newborn relationship" has to be nurtured with unconditional love and intuitive sensitivity on her part. The results will be much more satisfactory than if she gives in to her own hurt inner child, where two unconscious, unhappy "children" would be trying to connect. It is impossible to build a positive relationship when both people are regressed. This doesn't work in the adoptive relationship, and it won't work in the reunion relationship.

It is because of his regression that the birthmother, no matter how much she is feeling her own pain, must not burden the "child" with it, but must be there to listen to, acknowledge, and comfort *him.* She can tell him her story, the history of his conception and birth and her feelings about it, but need not go on and on about it. She need not apologize every time she sees him for having left him all those years ago, nor tell him over and over again how much she regrets not having been able to nurture him all those years. This may make sense to the adult person that he is, but it will not register very much on the feeling level of the child he now feels himself to be in his relationship to her.

This does not imply that the birthmother should put aside her feelings. For too many birthmothers, the need to ignore her feelings was what she heard over and over again, as it was explained to her how selfish it was for her to even think of keeping her baby. Her intrinsic, instinctive sense of not wanting to separate from him was probably never validated and was instead ignored or vilified. Many of these women have never had any support for those feelings, which persist even unto today.

The birthmother certainly needs an outlet for her pain. This outlet may be in the person of a therapist, friend, or support group, rather than her child. Just as it is inappropriate for any of us as parents to emotionally overload our children with our pain as they are growing up, neither is it appropriate in the regressive relationship with the adult/child to do so. If the birthmother does so, what may happen is that the adoptee may begin to feel that he must take care of her (the "parentified child" with which so many therapists are familiar), and once again there is no one to take care of him—no one to understand his pain. Thus he will begin to close down again, and the relationship will begin to take on superficial overtones. On the adult level he can certainly hear and understand the painful feelings she had in relinquishing him, but on another level, on the baby level, he really doesn't care.

Genetic Sexual Attraction

This brings us to the issue of sexual feelings between mother and child, which are very strong, because they are primal. They may not be sexual in the same sense that they would be between two mature adults, but they are sensual and primal and are often confused with purely sexual sensations. Sensual/sexual feelings are natural to the early experience of babies and their mothers. Both boys and girls will experience these feelings, because babies are creatures of sensation. In the normal and natural holding and touching which follows birth, sensual or sexual-like feelings are aroused in both mother and child. This is especially true of nursing mothers.

When these feelings come up in the reunion experience, there is a real pull to act upon them, because it feels like the only way to get close enough. The "child" isn't actually a baby and can't really be in a symbiotic relationship with the mother, nor can he go back to the womb. The next best thing seems to be to get inside her somehow, and the only way a man/child knows how to do this is through sexual intercourse. Unfortunately, some unboundaried mothers allow this act to take place, because in many cases she feels sexually attracted to him, too, and wants to consummate this feeling.

The Incest Taboo

To engage in sexual intercourse with her child is no more acceptable at this time, however, than it would have been when he actually was a child. (Or no more acceptable than a therapist having sexual relations with a patient.) It is a betrayal of trust. It is sexual molestation. Sensual *feelings* and sexual *impulses* to satisfy them are natural and can be acknowledged, but they should *not* be acted upon. It is a boundary crossed. And it is always the parent-figure who must take responsibility for setting safe limits. No matter how much the adoptee pleads with the mother/father/therapist, no matter how much he/she pulls for it, sexual relations between parent-figures and children, regardless of age, should never happen. Just as in every case of incest, it will backfire someday, and all the work of processing the reunion may come apart at the seams.

The incest taboo is part of almost every society and exists for a reason, a reason based more on psychology than biology. (This is why any parent-figure's transgressing that boundary is a betrayal of trust, whether a biological relationship exists or not). Mothers and sons, fathers and daughters can surely hug one another, touch one another, hold one another, but it has to be safe, and *it is up to the parent* to keep it that way.

Sensual/sexual feelings also occur between mother and daughter, and this is also natural. This does not mean that one has suddenly become a lesbian. It simply means that one is re-experiencing those early wonderfully sensual feelings one had at the beginning of life, before that untimely separation brought them to an abrupt and premature end. I do have a suspicion, based on interviews with several lesbian adoptees, that part of what they are searching for in their lesbian relationships is a closeness with the feminine that was mother. Many of these relationships are more sensual and emotional than sexual, even though they are sometimes expressed sexually. This would be an interesting area for more study.

Sexual Feelings Between Biological Siblings

Sexual feelings are not limited to those between mother and child or father and child. Sometimes, especially when a sister or half-sister looks a great deal like the mother at the age when she gave birth to him, or if she looks like him, a brother/son will feel an almost overwhelming attraction to her. His sister may also feel attracted to him, or she may be scared by the intensity of his feelings toward her. (This is equally true of relationships where the adoptee is a girl or woman and the birth sibling a boy or man.) In either case, it is all right to have, feel, and talk about these feelings, but it is not all right to act upon them. In fact, if everyone could get over the embarrassment of it, it would be healthy to talk about the feelings, instead of acting as if they don't exist or acting on them in covert ways. Unacknowledged or unvoiced emotions have a great deal more power than those which are out in the open and discussed. Remember that these feelings are *normal*. As the relationship matures, the feelings will most probably become less intense and at some point resolve into more appropriate and manageable feelings of warmth and affection toward one another. Should the original, intense, and sexual feelings be acted upon, it would put a great deal of strain upon the relationship and may even cause it to end.

In any case, sensual/sexual feelings are natural between birth-mothers and their children, both male and female, between fathers and daughters, and between siblings. Because of the physical memory traces of infancy, in the regressive stage of the reunion the most intense sexual feelings will be between mother and child. In all cases of sexual feeling, it is up to the parents to keep expressions of love and affection safe and boundaried, free from sexual acting out. (Of course, if the parents do not do so, it will be up to the adoptee to keep the boundaries clear.) There does need to be a reconnection, a closeness among birth family members, but if it does not feel safe, the "child" will begin to distance himself in his relationship with his birth family, and an opportunity for healing will be missed.

Reunions as Reconciliation

If reunions are going to be vehicles for reconciliation, the process must be understood and honored. Because of the emotionally charged climate in which these reunions take place, it is often difficult for anyone to respond responsibly to what is going on. As one birth-mother pointed out to me, "Not only did my son go back to being an infant, but I found myself feeling as if I were 17 years old again." Confusion and vulnerability predominate, as both mother and child communicate their histories and feelings, and struggle to define their new relationship.

During the early stage of the reunion, it is best if the adoptive parents can back off and give the fledgling relationship an opportunity to develop without the added burden of worrying about their feelings or their place in this new development. There will be a time to bring them into the process, because they are a part of it, but the reunited pair need as much space as possible to go through the very difficult early regressive stage of their relationship and to experiment with the ways in which they can begin to relate as adults. Although it may be difficult for some adoptive parents to realize it, their own relationship with their shared child will be much stronger if they can do so. It would be unfair for them to threaten to withhold their love and acceptance as a means of creating distance between the birthmother and her child or as a lever for admittance into the relationship at this time. The "child" needs permission to pursue this new relationship in whatever way seems best, and he needs unconditional love from everyone in order to do so effectively.

The Hard-to-Reach Adoptee

Sometimes a reunion, which started off gloriously, begins to deteriorate to the point of an almost nonexistent relationship. Many birthmothers, themselves hurt and feeling rejected, don't know what to do at this point. Because of their own feelings of rejection, there is a tendency to want to "just forget it," to try to "get on with life." *She should not forget that she tried this once before.* It might help her to know that many adoptive mothers were for years faced with this same feeling of rejection. If she can appreciate that these mothers "hung in there" despite the pain they were suffering, she can then begin to realize that she can do the same for her testing-out child.

Remember that whatever the "child's" chronological age, he is going to act somewhat child-like with her for some time. If both mothers have done what I recommended in the last chapter, which is to own their own feelings, they can give support to one another at this trying time in the reunion process. The adoptive mother, who has suffered years of frustration in the bonding process with her adopted child, can give comfort to what the birthmother is experiencing. If the adoptive mother had an "easy" time of it, then she can be happy that the adoptee waited until he met his biological mother to act on these feelings (which he has had all along). In either case, the birthmother needs support at this time, and she also needs to *not* abandon her child. Although I recommend that at first the primary relationship be limited to the reunited pair, without interference from either adoptive or birth families, in a case where the adoptee is testing the birthmother, she needs support from both family groups. Adoptive parents who were themselves tested by the adoptee can empathize with and encourage the birthmother while the adoptee learns to trust the relationship.

Of course, in cases where the adoptive parents are against the reunion and, in fact, interfere in that process, the birthmother will have to go elsewhere for support. But an added bonus to having the adoptive parents as supporters is that the adoptee will see that his relationship with the birthmother is not hurting them or affecting their feelings toward him. This can only strengthen his relationship with them, as well as allow him to begin to trust the new relationship with his birthmother. Love breeds more love and closer ties to everyone, while suspicion and fear create an atmosphere of tension and animosity benefiting no one.

The Reluctant Birthmother

Sometimes the adoptee experiences a second rejection upon making contact with his birthmother. Nothing he says or does changes her mind about not wanting a relationship with him. Whether the birthmother is in a state of denial about her pain, or if she has some fear about other members of her family rejecting her if they find out her "secret," being rejected again is devastating for the adoptee. It is almost impossible for the one who is ready for the reunion to do very much about the one who isn't. Often the birthmother negates the importance of the birth bond and convinces herself that her child had a good upbringing and doesn't need her. This is rationalization. Her hesitancy is much more unconscious than that. She doesn't want to face her pain and has found an excuse not to do so. She needs to know, however, that her reluctance to relate to her adult child will affect him deeply. All the excruciating feelings of abandonment and loss, with accompanying physical symptoms of stomach pain, headaches, diarrhea, and so forth resurface. He regresses whether she re-enters his life or not.

I urge any birthmother reading this book to reconsider if she is disinclined for any reason to allow some kind of relationship with the child she surrendered. He needs this connection to feel whole, and so does she. The impact of that separation has affected her life as well as his, and both need to heal. She will experience pain, but no wound can heal unless it is opened up. Knowing that he is languishing for her today is going to affect her, even as she convinces herself that he doesn't really need her. He does.

The birthmother's fears that her other children will reject her if they find out about him are probably groundless. For one thing, they already know something has been amiss. It has been established that children are usually aware of "secrets," even if they don't know what the secrets are. Secrets affect all members of a family, whether they can name them or not. It is best to get things out in the open. In almost every case I have known, siblings have been very accepting of their brother or sister. In fact, in cases where the mother refuses to meet with the adoptee, siblings have established close, long-lasting relationships. And, although these relationships may help soften the blow of the mother's not wanting a relationship, the connection the adoptee wants most is that with his birthmother.

Yet if the adoptee has done everything in his power to get his birthmother to acknowledge him and relate to him in some way, he may want to contact his siblings instead. This is his right, whether the birthmother wants it or not. He did not ask to be cut off from his genealogy, and he can't be expected to accept it. If the siblings are adults, it is up to them to decide whether or not they want to establish relationships with him. The mother can't make that decision for them. These relationships, although not as powerful as that with the mother, can be very healing. And sometimes the rest of her children can convince the birthmother to change her mind about relating to the child she relinquished.

Tenacity, Patience, and Understanding in the Reunion Process

Reunions can, indeed, be a vital part of the healing process for all sides of the adoption triad. But for healing to take place, all must own their own feelings as well as acknowledge and accept those of the others. No one can be left out, because each has been a part of the process. Each needs to stop projecting and passing judgment and, instead, provide understanding and support for one another. There will be no understanding on the part of the general public or public officials unless there is first understanding and empathy within the triad.

Even with mutual support, the reunion process is often misunderstood and can be difficult. It is a slowly evolving process, which needs to be understood at every stage of development. This takes patience, tenacity, and the cooperation of everyone involved, but especially that of the two mothers. At the beginning of the reunion process, when the adoptee is regressed in his relationship to the birthmother, it will be important for her to be sure that she acts in a mature and responsible manner towards him. This includes keeping the environment safe from inappropriate behavior, as well as continuing to communicate with him, even though he may not be responding to her. He may be having all kinds of ambivalent feelings which he is trying to sort out. Just as I recommended in the case of the adoptive mother, the birthmother will find it much more effective to validate and honor his feelings than to defend against them. He has a right to his feelings. His bringing them to her demonstrates his faith in her ability to hear him, which in itself should be healing for her. Because of the inequality in the relationship, however, she does not have the right to reciprocate until he has sufficiently matured in his relationship

179

to her. This is difficult, and I do not want her to think that she cannot express her feelings, but she needs to do so with someone other than him, for his sake as well as for the sake of the relationship.

None of the participants in these reunions can expect to eliminate the scar left by the relinquishment/adoption process. They can, however, gain new attitudes toward their experiences and become vital and permanent aspects of one another's lives. This takes time; it takes patience; it takes understanding; and, above all, it takes unselfish, unconditional, sacrificial love.

CHAPTER 14

Empowering Ourselves

In writing about the primal wound, I want to reiterate that the original trauma is abandonment as experienced by the child. The problem is not adoption. Adoption has attempted, with greater or lesser degrees of success, to be the solution to a problem, the problem of unplanned pregnancies. This is assuming, of course, that adoption is seen as an institution which seeks parents for babies who have to be separated from their first mothers, and not as an institution which seeks babies for childless couples. We must keep this distinction clear, otherwise procuring babies will become a way of life, as I believe it already has in some instances. Babies should never be separated from their mothers unless it is absolutely necessary, because separation causes trauma, and trauma leaves the child wounded. The wound affects adoptees all their lives and greatly impacts their relationships with others as they go through the life cycle.

How does one counteract the effects of this wound? So far I have discussed ways in which adoptive parents can help heal their children, ways in which triad members can help one another heal, and ways in which society can become more informed and compassionate about all aspects of adoption. Yet one of the residues of abandonment is a perpetual feeling of being a victim, of being powerless, of being helpless to help oneself. The original wounding, being preconscious and preverbal for most adoptees, leaves them feeling at the mercy of everyone and everything. The adoptee reacts to his pain and deprivation in unconscious ways, often sabotaging himself and leaving others perplexed.

It would be wonderful if everyone could get the long-term therapeutic help it would take to overcome the effects of that pain. Unfortunately this is not possible for a great number of people. It is, then, one's relationship to others which can offer the best opportunity for healing. This does not mean that one's partner or friend should be expected to be a parent and make up for primal deprivation. It means that both partners cooperate in validating feelings, setting boundaries, and taking responsibility for their own actions. This takes a great deal of commitment and perseverance on the part of all involved.

Shunning the Victim Role

The first thing an adoptee (or birthmother or anyone who feels powerless) can do is to become sick and tired of being a victim, of feeling as if he has no power in his life. That feeling of helplessness and hopelessness, which is left over from his infant/child years, permeates his consciousness even today. He has to *want* to get rid of it. He has to want to take responsibility for himself and not blame everyone—the whole world—for what is happening to him. It is easier to just drift along like a cork on the sea, bobbing along wherever the tide of life takes him. In order to grow up, to become an adult, he will have to give up that old friend lethargy and take an active part in his own healing process. This takes effort, commitment, and energy. How does he begin?

Challenging Long-Held Beliefs

One of the hindrances to an adoptee's helping himself heal is his feeling of being undeserving, unworthy. This is not reality, it is belief, and beliefs need to be challenged. The adoptee is paralyzed by the belief that he was responsible for his own abandonment because he wasn't a good enough baby to keep. By believing this, he is giving the mother who left him omnipotent wisdom in having made this decision, when she was actually a confused, vulnerable, and often very young person acting from fear or other people's advice. What will it take to challenge the belief that "I was unwanted, therefore I am unworthy"? In most cases neither part of that statement is correct. Yet how many adoptees operate in their lives based on that very belief? To adoptees I say: Challenge this belief. Hold a baby. Ask yourselves how bad you think that baby can be. If it is bad, toss it in the wastebasket the way you've done yourselves. If you're angry at your birthmothers for abandoning you, *why do you keep abandoning yourselves?*

Birthmothers are not immune from this kind of belief system. Because they gave up a child, many birthmothers consider themselves bad mothers, undeserving of having another child or unable to be good mothers to their other children. This belief often persists, regardless of the knowledge of their circumstances at the time of giving birth or the coercive tactics used to get them to feel guilty for wanting to keep their babies. Whether a birthmother gave up her baby because she realized that she could not care properly for him or because others convinced her of this, she must understand that she did what she was capable of doing at the time. We could all live lives of regret if we were to dwell on the mistakes we have made in our lives. But regret is one of those useless occupiers of our time and energy which gain us nothing. A birthmother cannot change what happened, but she can forgive herself for her decision or let go of the guilt if she really had no control over that decision. Her present relationships depend upon her doing so successfully.

Allowing Feelings—Controlling Behavior

There are two things to address if one wants to begin to take his power back. The first has to do with experience: the loss, deprivation, abuse, or neglect one experienced as a child; and the second has to do with how one reacts to that experience: the lifetime habits which result from the experience. What are some of those habits?

The adoptee often sabotages anything good that is happening to him. That sense of being undeserving overrides the wish to have some satisfaction in life. A good relationship turns into a nightmare because of childish responses to a partner. There is a sense of not being able to control those responses. This is because they are really reactions, behaviors over which we exercise no control. And yet, don't we expect our children to begin by age two or three to control their behavior? I've seen some parents acting more out of control than their children when trying to get their children to stop acting up. It's amazing! We all need to watch ourselves. I know I had to. In the beginning, before I understood what was going on with my daughter, I definitely used to react to her, rather than respond maturely to her. This only reinforced her faulty beliefs about herself, rather than challenging them and helping her heal. I was reacting from my own hurt inner child, rather than from the mature adult that I purported to be when I promised to parent my daughter. In order to keep my promise, I needed to grow up and take responsibility for my own actions.

This isn't easy. Others engender emotions in us which make it difficult to overcome the tendency to react, rather than to respond. For instance, adoptees use projective identification, not only as a defense mechanism and a primitive form of object relations, but also as a means of communication. What that means is that anyone in a relationship with him will begin to experience his feelings and react to them. The adoptee uses projective identification to communicate what he really feels inside because he has no words to describe those feelings. The feelings originated before he had language. Adoptive parents are very familiar with the technique of projective identification, as are reunited birthmothers, although they may not have known what it is called. Those projected feelings trigger the parents' own sense of rage, hostility, sorrow, or helplessness, causing them to react in ways they consider totally out of character for them.

But there is another reason for our allowing our behavior to get out of hand: Acting out is exciting! There is a sense of drama, a kind of negative excitement. Although it is a neurotic way to respond to hurt, fear, anger, or guilt, it keeps the drama in our lives going. It is dysfunctional, self-perpetuating, and an old friend without which we would feel depressed. It is the way in which we avoid growing up and taking responsibility for our choices and our actions. "I can't help it," is the way we put it. Well, we can't help the feelings; they come from the unconscious or from projection, but we can help the behavior. Often the behavior is drama, not a true response to feeling. Controlling our behavior takes a great deal of effort, but we can do it. We have to control our behavior in the case of unspeakable anger when we feel as if we could kill someone. We do (most of us) manage not to commit murder. But we allow ourselves the smaller indulgences of our neurotic reactions to archaic feelings. We slam the door, kick the dog, slap a child, yell at our husband or wife, or give the finger to the blankety-blank who cut us off on the freeway. It's exhilarating and dramatic! It feels good. That's the part that's hard to give up. But it's also childish—a two-year-old having a tantrum.

When those feelings overwhelm us, we need to ask ourselves: "Are these feelings appropriate to the situation I'm now in, or are they out of proportion to what is going on?" Many times it will be apparent that the feelings are too intense for the particular situation we're in. Then what we have to do is allow ourselves to experience the feeling, but *respond to the situation.* This is difficult because of the exhilarating feeling one gets when acting on intense feelings. We can't expect other people in our lives to put up with this kind of behavior, however. "He has to accept me as I am," is often what I hear. But one has to realize two things: that what one is demonstrating is behavior, not personality—not who one is; and that, in fact, *other people* **do not** *have to accept that behavior.*

185

The Difference Between Personality and Behavior

I'm sure every child at one time or another has been told, "I still love you; it is your behavior that I don't like." Whereas it may not have seemed to make much sense then, it actually does make sense. Personality is the essence of a person, the aspects which make one unique and which are present from birth. Behavior, on the other hand, is a form of communication—an attempt to tell someone something. Frequently the behavior is not congruent with the true personality. Behavior often reflects and projects pain. As we begin to become adults and accept responsibility for ourselves, we can begin talking about our pain with someone we love and trust, rather than acting it out. This implies, of course, that the listener will neither discount nor judge what we are saying. This takes a great deal of patience when a person is trying to verbalize primal feelings.

When an infant's needs were not met the way he wanted them to be, as is the case of a baby growing up in a family where there is no genetic connection, there is perpetual yearning to get those needs met by someone. There is a wish to go back to the symbiotic phase between mother and infant when a mother simply knows her child's needs and fulfills them. A baby separated from his mother at birth never had the security of that phase of life when his feelings were met in a fluid symbiotic dance with the mother. This leaves him with a never-ending longing to have that experience.

What happens in relationships is that he then expects his partner to just know what he needs or wants without his having to say anything. There is an expectation that his friend or wife or partner can read his mind. "It doesn't count if I have to tell her. She should just know what I want," is what one often hears. This is magical thinking. It isn't going to happen. It is an immature expectation which leaves both partners feeling angry. Even if a person were to get some of those needs met, they cannot be met in adulthood the same way that they would have been met in infancy. An adult doesn't need another person for survival. That particular phase of life is lost forever, and the realization or the denial of that loss causes a great deal of suffering. Realization initiates true grieving, while denial and avoidance become neurosis.

Acknowledging and Mourning Loss

Carl Jung said that neurosis is a substitute for legitimate suffering. Suffering involves acknowledging our losses and doing the appropriate griefwork. In his book *How to Be an Adult,* David Richo says, "Our problem is not that as children our needs were unmet, but that as adults they are still unmourned." Sadly, at some point in one's life it is necessary to face this truth and begin the mourning process. After many failed attempts, it becomes apparent that it is unreasonable for one to expect the adults (or even more so, the children) in our lives to make up for the primal needs of childhood. Yet many people in relationships try over and over again to do just that. The result is that *very few adult relationships are mature relationships.*

Every adoptee, birthmother, and adoptive parent has experienced loss, and the appropriate response to loss is mourning. Richo says that there is a need to grieve "the *irretrievable* aspect of what we lost and the *irreplaceable* aspect of what we missed." If we don't mourn our losses, if we don't realize that it is unreasonable and even impossible to expect our parents or partners to make up for these losses, we will go through life with "a feeling of something undone, a yearning for something unattained." There will be a sense of being the eternal victim, a feeling of powerlessness which prevents our growing up and being an adult.

There are several steps toward the healing power of griefwork. The first step is to want to grow up. Many people avoid responsibility and pain by remaining a victim. It is easier to keep the status quo. If we do decide that we are tired of always feeling powerless, the next step is to remember as much as possible about our painful experiences and to talk about them. It isn't always possible to remember cognitively, but we can take cues from our bodies, from our reactions to others, from our sense of something's being wrong.

Once we begin paying attention to the signals that we may be remembering a painful experience, we can then acknowledge the pain it caused us and begin to experience and express the feelings it induced in us. Instead of staying stuck in the drama of the feeling, we need to acknowledge the loss involved. That includes the realization that we are never going to get what we lost or never got, because we are no longer children and cannot receive as children. We can, however, speak up and directly confront those who caused us pain, or some representative of those persons. And we can begin to correct false beliefs about what happened. We will have to drop the expectation that others will fulfill our needs, and begin to fulfill them ourselves.

One of the ways in which we can mutually share our feelings with a partner is an exercise in Maggie Scarf's book *Intimate Partners*. I especially like this exercise, because it is a wonderful way to become more intimate and, paradoxically, more individuated in the relationship. A couple should set aside a certain amount of time, perhaps only half an hour at first, during which they will not be interrupted. They will need a timer, and each person will be allotted fifteen minutes in which to talk about him or herself. Each is to talk only about himself, not about the other or about the relationship. While one person is speaking, the other is to listen empathically, without judgment and without comment. At the end of fifteen minutes, they switch roles. They are not to go over the allotted time nor speak about what was said at a later date. These experiences should just be heard and accepted, never corrected, discussed, or analyzed because that would destroy trust and detract from the beneficial aspect of sharing important emotional experiences and feelings. If the couple continues with this exercise, each will learn something he or she did not know about the other person (with whom they may have been living for a long time!). This makes one's partner seem more real and unique, a separate person with different experiences. At the same time it will foster a feeling of closeness, connection, and intimacy. It is a way to begin the healing of loss and alienation.

When a person believes that he has remembered as much as is necessary about a difficult loss, it is helpful to have a ritual to symbolize the closure of the ways he has allowed that loss to impact his life. Each person has to find the best means of commemorating the releasing of the shackles of that loss by writing about it, painting it, sculpting it, etc., then burying or burning the symbol, and saying Goodbye.

When one has finally laid to rest the paralyzing effect of loss by remembering it, talking about it, then destroying it, it will be time to find a means by which to take one's power back. It must be remembered that it is because of a long-held belief that that power was given up. That belief is often based upon loss and involves fear. In the case of adoptees, it is the loss of the mother and the fear of another abandonment. This fear persists into adulthood, even though one cannot be abandoned as an adult. One can be left, but one cannot be abandoned because this implies helplessness at being left. One can *feel* helpless, but *as an adult one is not helpless*. An adult has many resources and can live by those resources. He will not die.

Three Barriers to Integration

The problem is that the adoptee's fear that he will die doesn't go away just because intellectually he knows that he can survive. Fear is one of the barriers to the integration of loss. The other two are anger/rage and guilt/shame. Each of these beliefs or feelings has both a true and a false aspect (or a justifiable and a neurotic component). The neurotic aspects are those which were formed in childhood in response to some experience which seemed dangerous, frustrating, or shameful. When a partner acts toward the adoptee (or anyone) in a hostile, hurtful, or unhelpful way, something gets triggered, an alarm goes off, and he experiences the fear of annihilation. Overcoming his response to that fear is an important part of the maturation process.

Fear

Fear can be an ally as a response to a dangerous situation. Justifiable or appropriate fear is that which appears when a real danger exists. We react to that fear by either fighting or fleeing. It gets the adrenaline going and helps us challenge whatever is endangering us, or to run from it. Neurotic fear, on the other hand, paralyzes us and hampers our life's work and our relationships. We may feel like fighting or fleeing, but can never act on either because there is no identifiable danger. In many cases, especially in the case of primal wounding, the danger is long past, or as Heidegger said, "The dreadful has already happened." Yet we keep reacting to stimuli which recreate the feelings that we had long ago. We have not integrated the original trauma, so the feelings keep getting triggered. We may not be able to stop the triggers, but we can learn to respond differently to those triggers.

Neurotic fear is the fear of what *might* happen. There is no immediate danger, only potential danger. In order to maintain this type of fear, we use rationalizations to invent possible objects for that fear. Adoptees will say, "I can't allow myself to get close to anyone, because I *might* be rejected." Richo gives three ways in which rationalizations maintain fear:

- The reason is meant to keep us in control by protecting us from surprises. This control backfires by vitiating our own resilience, a prerequisite for the integration of fear.

- The reason blockades access to adult solutions. We are so attached to a long-held belief that we lose perspective and mobility for change.

- The reason directly maintains the inertia of fear since we go on fearing what we refuse to confront.

Richo goes on to say, "The irony in all three of these is that what is meant to protect us *from* fear only protects the fear itself. Rationalization is the sentry that guards not us but the fear in us!"

Guilt/Shame

The second barrier to integration and wholeness is guilt. Guilt is not a feeling, but a judgment against ourselves. Guilt, too, comes in two varieties. Justifiable guilt is what one experiences when one has harmed another person or engaged in unethical conduct. It is information that what we did was wrong. When that happens we can make amends and try to avoid repeating the offense. Appropriate guilt is governed by our conscience and makes us accountable for our choices and actions. We can regain a sense of balance by admitting our guilt and making restitution. We can then forgive ourselves and be forgiven by others. There is a sense of integration and closure.

Neurotic guilt, on the other hand, is guilt about something over which we had no control. It leads to blame, not accountability. Instead of leading to reconciliation and integration, it leads to inner conflict and confusion. It cannot be resolved, because either it has no cause in the present or it is a cover-up for other feelings such as sorrow or anger.

Shame is different from guilt. We feel guilty for what we did or imagined that we did; we feel shameful for who we are. It is the difference between *doing* and *being*. Shame serves no useful purpose, because it cannot be integrated. It tells us that we are not worthy. It lowers our self-esteem and sabotages our sense of Self. This is the judgment or belief that many adoptees have about themselves because they were given up for adoption. They couldn't have *done* anything too terrible, since they were so small, so that means that they must have *been* terrible. They need to remember to ask themselves: How terrible can a baby really be?

If a birthmother feels shame, it is probably from some early belief about herself, not because of the relinquishment. Relinquishment is an act, which might lead to guilt. Guilt is one of the things which many adoptees say get in the way of their relationships with their birthmothers after reunion. An adoptee can never really talk to his birthmother about his true feelings, because that brings up his mother's guilt, and then he has to take care of her. Sometimes her guilt is a mask for intense feelings, such as anger or sorrow. It disguises her lack of control over something that happened to her. Having a semblance of control, even if it means experiencing guilt, sometimes seems preferable to feeling as if she had no control, or experiencing the painful truth of her situation.

In order to be healed from the paralyzing effects of guilt, we must first ascertain whether it is an appropriate adult response to a hurtful deed, or if it is a neurotic means by which we deny truth, avoid responsibility, or mask a more painful feeling. We will have to determine whether what we are experiencing is guilt or shame. Then we will be able to resolve the conflict and promote healing. *The healing for guilt is forgiveness; the healing for shame is acceptance.*

Anger/Rage

A third barrier to positive relationships is anger. Again, we are not talking about legitimate anger at something that someone did to us. That kind of anger is appropriate and can lead to resolution. I am talking about that overwhelming anger that seems to come out of nowhere and which either explodes onto the scene or is so buried that it makes one numb. I am talking about infant rage.

This rage seems so powerful to the person who suspects that it lurks within him that he often fails to feel it at all. Other people always seem to be angry at everyone and everything. Sometimes anger is genuine and other times it is histrionic. The histrionic anger is more drama than true feelings and does nothing toward integration. If anger is real and justified, then expressing it at the appropriate person in an appropriate way will dissipate it and release us from the tension of it. One cannot hang on to true anger. It is a very brief feeling.

Anger is also a great motivator. It can get one going toward righting societal or personal wrongs. It releases a great deal of energy; it stimulates power; it can point one toward assertiveness, so long as it is appropriate to the situation. If it is inappropriate, it will stimulate aggression, which is an attempt to control or intimidate others. Or it can lead to passivity, which is another form of control, controlling by what one *doesn't* do.

Taking Back Our Power

Having examined some of the most common hindrances to integration and wholeness—the beliefs that keep us from assuming our own power—we can look at ways to begin taking our power back. By power I mean "power within" not "power over." *Power within* makes us feel calm and whole. It allows us to be assertive, but not aggressive. *Power over* is a form of aggression, intimidation, and control over others. When one has true power, it makes us free, whereas always feeling the need to control others takes away our own power. True power involves taking responsibility for our choices and actions; it involves establishing and maintaining boundaries; it involves inviting change; and it involves taking risks.

Many of these innovative changes overlap when we begin to implement a new attitude toward old experiences. Challenging our old belief system is not as easy as it sounds. Those beliefs are familiar, they're old friends. It is difficult to let go of them. It is important to take small steps toward change. The exercise given earlier in this chapter is a good way to begin. It is a relatively safe way to show feelings to ourselves and to others, an important step toward wholeness.

Part of discovering the true self is knowing our own values, ideas, and opinions, and being able to express them and hold onto them in the face of differing viewpoints and without having to convince others that we are right. It also means keeping an open mind and being willing to change our ideas based on new and better information, not on the need for approval.

The flip side of holding on to our own values and opinions is to check out our assumptions, suspicions, and doubts about others, rather than acting from our own perceptions. Perceptions are colored by our own experiences and are never truly objective. They are also influenced by our personalities, the way in which we function in the world. We need to check out our assumptions, because misunderstandings can lead to alienation and rejection. Communication is an important aspect of testing the validity of our perceptions.

Often we allow others' behavior to influence the way we act. This, again, may be because of false assumptions. Or it may be that we are personalizing everything that happens to us. We assume that another's behavior says something about us, instead of seeing it as information *about him*. A person may even go so far as to assume that someone cutting him off on the freeway is actually doing something *to him*! Since the driver has probably never seen him before, why would he want to do something to him? He is simply driving recklessly. This is information about the driver, not a personal affront to the one being cut off. How many times have you taken another person's mistake for a personal attack on you? If we want to stop giving others control over us, we can stop reacting to their behavior and simply see it as information.

This brings us to mistakes, our own mistakes. One of the changes we need to make if we are to be more whole is to take risks. Taking a risk implies not knowing the outcome of our actions. This means that we are going to make mistakes. What are mistakes? Mistakes are risks taken that didn't work out. We can do something differently next time. Mistakes give us another way of gaining information. As children, we may have feared that our parents wouldn't approve of us if we made mistakes. That may or may not have been a true evaluation of the situation. Now, however, we need to approve of ourselves, so we can forgive ourselves our mistakes and just accept the lesson they teach us. Someone gave me this saying: "Far better to dare mighty things, even though checked with failure, than to live in the grey twilight that knows not victory or defeat."

One of the risks we have to take if we are to become more integrated is the risk of intimacy. Many people have little sense of their own boundaries, because they grew up in a home where boundaries were diffuse. It is impossible to feel safe in a relationship unless we can know that we won't get lost in it. There has to be a balance between closeness and separation, relationship and individuation. Children practice this when they are between the ages of eighteen months and two years, when they toddle away from mother, then come back to make sure that she is there. They feel safe going away from her only if they know that she will be there when they return. The mother's ability to allow the child to safely explore new territory without the mother's being over-anxious, and her willingness to allow the child to return safely to her loving embrace fill the child with the measure of confidence needed for healthy relationships in the future. If the mother cannot negotiate that period safely for her child, he may forever feel either engulfed or abandoned in his relationships with others.

Empowering ourselves is like a double-edged sword. On one side is freedom, freedom from our need for approval and the constant concern about what others think about us; on the other side is the necessity to take responsibility for our feelings and our choices. We no longer have to fear others, but neither can we blame them. We must withdraw our projections and own our own feelings, then act responsibly in the ways in which we express them. Again, we see how paradoxical life is—and how balanced!

Being Assertive

Being assertive means taking care of ourselves. It does not mean being intrusive or intimidating. As I have stated before, it is having power within oneself, not power over others. A great deal of the time it is not that others want to take power away from us, but that we give up that power. Donna, an adoptee from Florida, told me that an adoptee is a person who, when someone steps on his toes, says, "Excuse me," instead of "Ow." The idea that one is undeserving is based on a perception of an early experience. It is time to challenge this belief. As we begin to ask directly for what we want or need, we must also be ready to accept that not everyone can meet those needs. Accepting disappointment is part of becoming mature.

Being assertive means being clear; it doesn't necessarily mean being sure. Being assertive may mean saying, "I'm not sure; let me think about that." At the same time that we must be able to ask for our needs to be met, we must also be able to say "No" to what we don't want.

Some people may be angry at the implication that they can change simply by a change in attitude or behavior. It will seem too simple. And they are right. It is not simple or easy. Those archaic feelings and our responses to them will not just spontaneously disappear. But if one doesn't have the time, money, or courage to get long-term professional help, there is a need to begin acting "as if," to take a risk, then check the results. Sometimes the results will be good and sometimes they will be disappointing. Accepting that one's needs or wishes will not always be met is the mature way to react to risk-taking.

The wounds of early childhood are often repressed and inaccessible to conscious memory, yet they affect us in myriad ways throughout our lives. One of the reasons for this life-long effect is the beliefs we have about the sources of those wounds, which we frequently attribute to ourselves—the bad child within. Do we really want to continue letting these beliefs manipulate us, or can we be willing to opt for a better, more mature, but less familiar way to conduct our lives? We don't need everyone to love us. What we do need is a sense that we are real. Only false selves have no enemies. Only ineffective people cause no controversy. Only fear based on archaic feelings will keep us from finding our sense of Self. And only we can make the difference. Nothing is going to change unless we make it change. Deciding not to act is a choice. As Richo says, "Remember that what we are not changing, we are choosing."

Finding a Spiritual Path

One of the casualties of being disempowered by abandonment is a spiritual perspective. Many adoptees have told me that they find it difficult to believe in a God who allows babies to be separated from their mothers. It violates their sense of order in the universe, replacing order and meaning with chaos and terror. There is a sense of being a mistake, of having no right to exist in the world. There is no sense of belonging in the family into which they were placed, that into which they were born, or in the universal schema.

This sense of not belonging causes a spiritual dilemma. Although many adoptees have found comfort in religion, for others there is the same falseness about religion that they find in the rest of their lives. There is a sense that what is going on is not meant for them, that they are frauds in the inner sanctum of religious rites, ceremonies, or rituals, and that at any moment they may be found out.

Birthmothers, too, have difficulty reconciling their religious beliefs —those they grew up with—with a sense of betrayal by both their parents and the church at getting no support in their dilemma. Some of this doubting may be the result of the judgmental attitudes many religious organizations demonstrate toward unwed mothers. The judgmental, vindictive, punitive attitudes which shame mothers into giving up their babies also spill over into attitudes toward the offspring of those mothers. The feeling of the mother is "I made a mistake"; the feeling of the child is "I *am* that mistake." Both the mothers and their children doubt their own goodness, their own acceptance in the world.

These moral attitudes may have to do with power, the need for one group of people to exercise control over another. In such cases, if we can separate the spiritual aspect of life from the religious aspect; or if we can determine that man, not God, is making these judgments against us, perhaps we can see that there is a place for all of us in the universal order of things—that there are no mistakes in that schema. All religions have discriminated against certain groups of people at some time in history: women, Blacks, gays, Jews, etc.; yet we all belong to the Family of Man—we are all related; we are all equal. Man is not God, goddess, life-force, or higher power, and we need not let man determine our relationship to that higher being.

Everyone seeks meaning in life. Some people will be able to reconnect with the religion of their childhood or join another. Other people may want to follow a more personal spiritual path. It is possible to begin to believe in the rightness of things, in the legitimacy of being, and to follow a spiritual path which allows for this belief. The universal law is love, and there is no one from whom this love is to be withheld. Children begin to experience a spiritual sense in their connection with natural wonders. For those who are having existential or spiritual difficulties, perhaps that is the place to begin. We can all smell a flower, touch a tree, observe a butterfly, and look up at the stars to find a place in the natural order, a connection to the cosmos. We can find our place in the universe.

PART FOUR

Conclusions

CHAPTER 15

Further Implications of the Primal Wound

The Impact of Abandonment on Other Populations

Because my particular hypothesis raises many philosophical and social, as well as psychological dilemmas, I will try to answer some of the questions put to me during the course of my research. Although this book has been written for and about members of the adoption triad, it has implications for people other than those involved with adoption.

There are many ways in which a child can be abandoned, and many people have written to tell me that they were not adopted, but that much of what I have to say also applies to them. Children who have spent the first days, weeks, or months of their lives separated from their mothers by being placed in incubators may experience the same symptoms which relinquished babies experience. In addition, these children have to contend with visceral, cellular, and emotional feelings of painful medical procedures, many of which were performed without the benefit of anesthesia, and which remain as somatic memory traces. The medical profession has either misunderstood or chosen to ignore the sensitivity of these babies to the emotional pain of separation from mother or the physical pain of medical procedures. Expediency, convenience, technology, and profit often take precedence over the aspects of healing which include compassion, empathy, kindness, and mercy. Concern for the well-being of the whole person is lost. The mind/body split still operates in many of our hospitals and doctors' offices today.

Children growing up in alcoholic or drug-addicted families, children whose parents are themselves suffering from some generational family dysfunction in which the parents are emotionally absent from their children, and children of divorce—all of these will in one way or another exhibit some of the problems which have been outlined here.

One group which is difficult to talk about, but which may have a significant impact on society in the near future, is the group of children who are literally growing up in day care centers. The need for women to work, plus women's wanting to exercise their hard-won place in the work force, may be placing children at risk. Women certainly have a right to be whatever they want to be, but not at the expense of their children. When one gives birth or adopts a baby, there is then a responsibility to nurture and care for the child. Having someone else do it, in my opinion, compromises the emotional health of the baby. This almost always means that parents have to make some sacrifices for their child.

Do I think that the primary caretaking responsibility belongs more to the mother than to the father? Yes, at least during the first couple of years. Everything I have discovered about the profound, primary connection between mother and child underscores the child's critical need for his mother. During infancy, I believe no one else can truly take the place of the mother, and that her absence will have a tremendous impact on the child. Some women may resent my placing so much of this responsibility upon them, yet I will stand by this position, both as a mother and as a psychotherapist. We need to make choices, and some of those choices have to do with what we are willing to sacrifice for our children. *Denying a mother's importance to her children will not diminish or erase that importance.* A child's sense of security probably has very little to do with his or her socio-economic status. Rather, his sense of security may hinge on his very early relationship with his mother and his subsequent relationship with both parents.

Many, many women recognize and agonize over this conflict. What can they do if they simply can't stay home? They can allow their children to complain about it, and acknowledge their feelings without becoming defensive about it themselves. They know in their hearts that quality time is not the hour between seven and eight at night or a Saturday afternoon. Quality time for a child is having mother available when he wants her, day or night. If mother is not available, it will bring up feelings for the child, feelings that the mother will have to be prepared to acknowledge and validate.

We will have to examine the impact of our decisions upon ourselves and our children. Just because we have no choice doesn't mean that our children have no feelings. "I can't help it" is not a reason to silence our children. When we do that, we miss a wonderful opportunity to understand our children and to soothe them. And they begin to comprehend that talking about feelings is not all right, and that perhaps even having feelings is not all right. Children need to be able to talk about their feelings, so that the feelings don't become bigger than life or repressed. Listen to your children today, so they won't have to pay a therapist to do so fifteen or twenty years from now!

I also believe that fathers are *very* important in the lives of children and can certainly take over much of the caretaking at some point. My belief that all children have a right to have both parents in their lives puts me at odds with some single women who want to have children without acknowledging the biological father or without having a male influence in the life of their child. There is often a vindictive quality to this practice which needs to be explored by the women, and for which the child should not have to suffer. This may be especially difficult for boys, who need to identify with their fathers (although women tell me, "We need our fathers, too!"). Men are beginning to acknowledge the pain they feel about the absence of a father in their lives as they were growing up.

Related to this issue is the practice of using *anonymous* donors for sperm banks, which I believe should be abolished. Artificial insemination, when necessary, may be all right, but not if the donor, whether it be a sperm or egg donor, wishes to remain anonymous. No one should be anonymous. Everyone has a right to know his or her biological heritage.

In addition to not knowing who one's biological parents are, there is the problem of multiple sperm or eggs being donated by a single person. This brings up the possibility of inbreeding. Genetic sexual attraction, explained in the chapter on reunions, doesn't happen only in adoptive situations. It happens in many families, because we are attracted to those who look like us or are in some way familiar to us. It is like falling in love with the other half of ourselves. Oedipus Rex will live again, because if someone is not marrying his mother, he may indeed be marrying his sister. This promises to become a big problem for "anonymous" people and needs to be addressed. There may be a day when DNA tests will be required for obtaining marriage licenses! We now have such a wide array of options for childless couples, such as surrogacy, IVF, anonymous sperm banks, egg donors, and so forth, that the possibilities for psychological trauma are staggering.

The Surrogacy Myth

As far as surrogacy is concerned, it should first be noted that the wrong mother is labeled the surrogate in this practice. A woman who gives birth to a baby *is* the mother of that baby, not a surrogate mother. The surrogate is the substitute mother, the one who acts in place of the mother, or in this case, the adoptive mother for whom the misnamed "surrogate" is giving birth.

This distinction is very important, because it may be this complete reversal of truth which has given an air of legitimacy to the surrogacy program. If we call the real mother the surrogate mother, it makes it easier to deny her importance in her child's life. As my thesis sets forth, infants separated from their mothers suffer a narcissistic wound. Therefore it would seem obvious that to conceive a child with the *intention* of separating from that child would be setting the child up for psychological distress. These mothers are not deliberately setting out to harm their children; they are just unaware of what the consequences will be when that connection is severed. (Or, as in the case of Baby M and many others, if they change their minds and want to keep their babies, they are considered unstable!) In some recent cases, surrogacy contracts have been given preference over the instincts of mothers who have changed their minds early in the pregnancy. If contracts for human life take precedence over maternal instincts and the psychological well-being of children, we are in trouble as a society.

I have given a great deal of thought to the question of which is the "real" mother in the case of a surrogate carrying the biological child of another woman. In this instance, the surrogate is impregnated with the other woman's egg, which may be fertilized with her husband's sperm or the sperm of a donor. The "surrogate" or gestating mother in this case is not the biological mother. Would this make a difference in the impact of separation from her on the child? I don't think so. I think that the profound connection is in the prenatal bonding and that the emotional trauma of separation will occur even when the child is in no way genetically connected to the gestating mother. Children are as genetically connected to their fathers as to their mothers, yet separation from father is not a trauma to a newborn. That connection is established later. Since the child will have a genetic connection to both of his biological parents, they, too, will play a part in his understanding of himself. Whether he is separated from the mother who carried him in her womb for nine months or from the biological mother, the child will probably suffer some kind of trauma.

The Need for Integrity

We now have the technical capabilities to create families in a variety of ways. In vitro fertilization has made it possible for many previously infertile couples to bear children. As long as the mother and child are not separated and the father is known and preferably present in the family, this is, to me, a better method of having a child than surrogacy. Whatever the method, however, we have to be aware of the consequences of what we are doing. Unfortunately, in many cases, *our technical abilities greatly exceed our moral integrity*, so that we remain in denial about the impact of our endeavors. Or, as Ian Malcolm, a character in Michael Crichton's thriller *Jurassic Park*, says "Scientists are actually preoccupied with accomplishment. So they are focused on whether they *can* do something. They never stop to ask if they *should* do something." We need to begin to ask ourselves, just because we *can* do something, does that mean that we *should*? This question is going to be very important in the next couple of decades. We must not lose sight of the effect our manipulation will have on the "products" of that technology. The upcoming fields of molecular biology and genetic engineering, which for the most part remain unregulated, will need the influence of intelligent, honest, compassionate, and highly principled people if we are to evolve into a society made up of emotionally and spiritually healthy individuals.

The Wicked Stepmother

One of the comments made to me by adoptive mothers is that they feel like a wicked stepmother in their relations with their adopted children. No matter what they do, they are perceived as being to blame for everything that goes wrong in their children's lives. All the wicked stepmother stereotypes come to mind. The wicked stepmother is a frequent character in fairy tales. In this day of divorce and the breaking up and blending of families, we hear a lot about stepparenting. Much of what is said about the stepmother could also be said about the adoptive mother. It may not be that she is either wicked or hateful to the child, but that *she is just the wrong mother.* So to the child she becomes dark, wicked, or ominous.

I remember a talk show program in which several children were on stage with their fathers and stepmothers. The host kept emphasizing to the children how hard these substitute mothers were trying "to be there" for them, to help them, and to love them; yet the children would not accept them in the way that the stepmothers wanted to be accepted. No one was "getting it," least of all the host, who accused one little boy of just trying to exert power over his family. No one understood that it wasn't about the stepmother's not being a good person; it was just that the child wanted his or her own mother. No one else would do, no matter how wonderful she was. Most children of divorce want nothing more than for their parents to get back together so that the family can be whole again. The new wife, the stepmother, is a hindrance to this happening.

This scenario also gets played out with adoptees, although it is much less conscious. Even though most adoptive parents come into the adoption picture with a sincere desire to do what is best for the child, in the unconscious of the child there is a memory of the other mother and a desire to be with her. The adoptive mother seems like a hindrance to the child's reuniting with his first mother. In some cases the child actually feels stolen by the adoptive parents. An adoptive mother may get caught up in the difficulty her child has in accepting her, feel rejected, and act inappropriately toward him. Her behavior plus the child's unconscious knowing that this is the "wrong" mother give rise to the image or archetype of the wicked stepmother. At the same time, the child fears that this mother, too, might abandon him; the anxiety goes up, the acting out increases, the adoptive mother reacts, and she looks even more like the wicked stepmother.

Of course there are adoptive parents, just as there are non-adoptive parents, who are so dysfunctional themselves that they cannot put their child first. But often the perception on the part of the adoptee that the adoptive mother is some manifestation of the wicked stepmother needs to be reexamined by him when he reaches adulthood. A great deal of projective identification goes on in adoptive homes. The provocation and outrageous behavior on the part of some adoptees has caused many a calm, sensitive mother to become a raging maniac. Had my daughter and I not been in therapy, she no doubt would have perceived me to be the Wicked Witch of the West. Had we not gotten help, I probably would have *become* the Wicked Witch of the West! I have encouraged adoptive parents to distinguish between behavior and personality when dealing with children; I would now like to encourage their grown children to do the same for them. Feeling rejected makes people do a lot of things they regret.

Fetal Alcohol Syndrome and the Adopted Child

For a long time adoptive parents have been puzzled by the aggressive behavior of some of their children and stymied as to what to do about it. Ever since Michael Dorris' book *The Broken Cord* came out, was made into a TV movie, and then featured on *20/20*, there has been a barrage of inquiries and letters from parents who are sure that their children are suffering from fetal alcohol syndrome. A disproportionate number of those letters are from adoptive parents. While it is no doubt true that some adopted children are victims of this disability, it is my belief that many of these children are instead suffering from the effects of separation from the birthmother. This wound may be exacerbated by FAS, but not all children who exhibit difficult behavior or problems in school are FAS children.

What seems to have happened is that adoptive parents, who have been noticing this behavior for years, have found something to "pin it on." These parents are now coming out of the closet, because there is now an "explanation" for the way their children are acting.

Previously, the only explanation seemed to be that they were not being good enough parents. Parents who had the courage to go to therapists for help were often blamed for their children's problems. Relatives, friends, and teachers criticized the parents, especially the mother, for not being firm enough, or for allowing the child to abuse them. With the advent of drug addicted or FAS babies, here at last was the explanation for the kinds of problems many parents had been afraid to talk about.

The danger in assuming this behavior is caused by FAS is that the parents might feel hopeless about helping their children, since there is no way to repair the neurological damage caused by FAS. It is very important to try to ascertain whether or not the birthmother did indeed drink during pregnancy, or if the child is instead suffering the pain of separation from her. It seemed apparent to me that Dorris' son Adam was suffering from both the primal wound and FAS. Informed consent—about FAS or other complications such as sexual abuse should be a law. This is not so that only "perfect" babies will be adopted, but so that children with problems can be helped.

Dorris' wife said something on the *20/20* segment which I think is significant. She said that it seemed as if a part of Adam's soul was missing. This is exactly what adoptees say to me, whether or not their mothers had been drinking. Dorris had no way of knowing that the primal wound was operating in Adam, because none of the "experts" to whom he took Adam for help ever suggested such a thing. Had he been aware of it, there may have been ways he could have validated Adam's feelings, even if he couldn't have taken away the neurological effects of the alcohol. He calls his book *The Broken Cord*, so perhaps on some level he suspects such a wound exists. Had the primal wound explanation been available, however, he might not have pursued the problem until he found out about FAS. The discovery of the effects of FAS will help many parents understand their children.

Alcoholism is a problem for many, many families, and birth-mothers are not the only women who drink during pregnancy. More studies need to be done on non-adopted victims of FAS in order to discover which symptoms are really related to FAS and which are primal wound issues that are complicated by FAS. There is work to be done!

The Question of Abortion

The question is often put to me: "If adoption is so difficult, would it be better for a woman to have an abortion?" This, like the issue of adoption, has no one right answer. It is, like much of life, paradoxical and deserves to be understood as such. Yet there is probably no subject today about which we are so polarized, neither side admitting the truths about the other's point of view or admitting the fallacies of its own. Many women, however, in their heart of hearts, have mixed feelings about abortion. They believe that the choice should be an option, but hope that they will never have to make that choice. What is definitely needed, just as in the case of adoption, is the opportunity to make an *informed* choice. This is difficult because of the blurring of the issues from both sides of the debate.

The belief that the being within the pregnant woman is, indeed, human life from the moment of conception has less to do with religion than with logic. What can the organism be if it is not a human being in its earliest stage of development? Before a woman seeks an abortion, she must first be pregnant. To be pregnant means to be "with child." Yet some pro-choice advocates make having an abortion sound like removing some appendage, some unnecessary part of the woman's own body. (One woman was told to think of it as if she were having her appendix removed!) The zygote/fetus is a separate entity which is *attached* to the woman's body, but is not *part of* her body. It is a separate being and it is alive. Birthmothers may also be familiar with the tactic of making something seem less traumatic than it actually is. Diminishing the impact of her decision, whether that decision is to abort or to relinquish, is dishonest and does not help a woman make an informed choice.

Somewhere deep within, a woman knows that she has begun to nurture a new life and that having an abortion means ending that life. She does not need someone trying to convince her that this is not true. What she does need is help in handling the emotional fall-out from her decision, so that she does not have to live a life of unconscious guilt. In her excellent book *Soul Crisis*, Sue Nathanson deals honestly and sensitively with the difficult decision to have an abortion. She was and is pro-choice, but unfortunately, at the insistence of some radical pro-choice people, this book was banned in at least one bookstore (in Berkeley, of all places!), because the author refused to make her abortion experience sound like having a tooth extracted. This attitude just gives fodder to the pro-life people, who are also dealing in partial truths.

Pro-lifers blithely advocate "adoption, not abortion," completely denying or ignoring the psychological consequences of that painful solution on either the mother or the child. Some pro-lifers actually recommend adoption over the mother's keeping the baby, because the baby was "conceived in sin"! This judgmental narrow-mindedness has caused many babies who may have been kept by their own mothers to suffer the trauma of that separation from her. If the zygote/embryo/fetus/baby is still psychologically part of the mother until some time after birth, that separation from her may feel like death. Putting a baby up for adoption may make some adoptive parents and pro-life advocates happy, but it may destine the child to a life of emotional turmoil.

Difficult Choices

There are no easy answers. We have strongly held beliefs, but we really don't know. It does seem as if each side of the abortion issue is in denial about what the other is saying. Pro-life people espouse the wonders of adoption, completely ignoring the pitfalls of this alternative, or the painful lives of unwanted children who daily suffer unspeakable atrocities at the hands of abusive parents. Pro-choice people often deny that what is being destroyed is life and that the mother is in fact a mother and will be impacted by choosing to abort, even if she manages to stay in denial for twenty years. Women who have had abortions and have also given up a child for adoption will most often say that adoption was the more difficult of the two for them to deal with, because the child is "out there" somewhere, and they have no idea what happened to him.

What do adoptees think? One of the first questions many of them ask their birthmothers upon meeting them for the first time is, "If abortion were an option then, would you have aborted me?" Or, the younger adoptees will ask, "Did you think about abortion when you learned that you were pregnant with me?" In neither case do they want the answer to be "Yes." Even though some adoptees have been in so much pain that they may have wished that they had been aborted, most of those with whom I've spoken are thankful that their mothers did not have an abortion. They may have problems, but they have life.

More Honesty and Support, Less Judgment

It is important to be honest with a woman who may be seeking an abortion about the fact that there is, indeed, life within her and that she may have some feelings about ending that life. We need to keep in mind that women who have had abortions need to mourn their loss, just as birthmothers do, and that society needs to help them do so. We can help first by recognizing that a life existed, then by showing compassion for the mother. There has to be a period of forgiveness and renewal after the grieving process has been completed, so that these significant life events do not paralyze or inhibit subsequent responses to the generative instinct or the parenting process.

Although women should have a choice about whether or not to carry a baby to term, it is a terrible choice, and we should do more to ensure that women do not have to make that painful choice. The alternatives should include the quaint idea of self-control or abstinence.

In addition to being a religious/moral issue, being sexually active is also a psychological/social issue. Just because a person is physically capable of having sexual intercourse does not mean that one is emotionally or psychologically ready for a sexual relationship. Many young people just want to feel loved. We are failing them in this. And we are failing to impart to them the tremendous emotional impact these kinds of decisions will have on the rest of their lives. If they do make a conscious choice to be in a sexual relationship, then they should have information and access to birth control methods and devices, so that their next decision does not need to be a life or death decision. If pregnancy does occur, there are three choices: keep the baby, have an abortion, or put the baby up for adoption. *All three choices will have life-long consequences for both mother and child.*

If a woman should decide to have an abortion, perhaps it would be best to err on the side of caution and make abortion procedures as humane as possible (for the developing fetus, as well as for the mother). There is now enough evidence of people being able to remember, through the use of hypnosis, attempted abortions, to make one stop to think that the least we can do is to anesthetize those involved in the abortion process and recognize the fetus as a human being whose feelings need to be honored. It has taken until 1992 for many in the medical profession to recognize that infants can feel medical procedures and that they do much better when fully anesthetized than when they have to feel the terrible pain of those procedures. How much longer are we going to remain in the dark about what the fetus feels? What do doctors suppose recoil action means anyway if it doesn't mean that something is painful, intrusive, or abhorrent to the organism? Perhaps detachment has replaced compassion in too many doctors' professional attitudes.

True Beliefs or Convenience?

Many of our beliefs are simply a matter of convenience. It is easier to believe that we can substitute mothers than to take the responsibility for believing otherwise. It is easier to believe that fetuses are not really human beings than to go through the conscious choice of ending a life. It is easier to believe that babies feel none of the medical procedures performed upon them than to take the precautions necessary to alleviate pain. It is easier to believe that turning over the rearing of our children to rotating nannies or day care providers will not harm them, than to put our careers on hold, stay home, and give up some of the material advantages of two incomes. It is easier to believe that our children are too young to remember and thus be hurt by sexual abuse than to leave the abusing parent.

It is time that we stop denying painful truths in order to avoid the painful work of making difficult decisions, decisions which affect the well-being of our children. Our failure to keep our children safe and secure puts them in a perpetual state of anxiety. It is time to listen to our children and to put their welfare ahead of our own. Adopted children, foster children, stepchildren, biological children—all children deserve nothing less than our very best love and protection.

CHAPTER 16

Honor Thy Children

Challenging Old Assumptions

There has been a general assumption on the part of many people that if a relinquished child is placed with adoptive parents early enough, he will not experience separation trauma. This is an assumption to which I have taken exception. Some of the research which I have used to challenge this assumption pertains to the importance of prenatal bonding, the physiological and psychological preparation for birth by the mother, the amazing awareness of infants at birth, and the significance of early postnatal bonding and imprinting experiences, which will be different for infants who experience a bonding continuum than for those who experience separation from the biological mother.

Another assumption, which is perpetuated by some social workers, adoption agencies, and other adoption facilitators is that if an adoptive couple loves a child enough, he will be fine. This places tremendous expectations upon both the adoptive parents and the child, because it completely ignores the idea that love is a form of communication, which has to be received as well as given. For a child who has been given up by the one person in the world from whom he might have been able to expect unconditional love, the ability to trust love from anyone else is, I believe, impaired.

The Mother Connection

There is an assumption inherent in my theory that the primary relationship is the one between mother and child. This assumption is based upon my understanding of the current research into prenatal physiological, hormonal, and psychological connections to the fetus in utero and of the subsequent part the mother plays as representative of the newborn's Self, as related by Neuman and by Mahler. It is understood that human beings are adaptable, but there is much that is yet to be learned about the cost of that adaptability so far as the substitution of mothers is concerned. This is especially true if that adaptation had to begin at the preconscious, preverbal stage of post-uterine life.

What this research implies to me is that the key to self-esteem may lie in the initial relationship of a child to his mother. This mother/child relationship seems to me to be so profound as to be mystical. The early bonding experience, a continuum between the prenatal and postnatal experience of the mother/child unity, suffusing the child with concomitant feelings of security, trust, and unconditional love, may go a long way toward sending a child on the path of self-esteem and self-worth.

Putting the Well-Being of the Child First

I believe that society would benefit from making sure that mothers who want to and are emotionally capable of caring for their children be encouraged and allowed to do so. It makes no sense to me that we take babies away from mothers who have no financial resources, and then *pay someone else* (foster parents) to take care of them. Why not pay the real mother? Some women are courageous enough to withstand the scorn of society and the humiliation by family members to go on welfare and keep their children. This is not easy because of the stigma attached to such an arrangement.

I know one such courageous woman. When she became pregnant she refused to give up her baby, even though her parents disowned her. She went on welfare for three years so that she could stay home with her baby and give her a good start in life. This was a humiliating experience for her, but she was willing to face the humiliation in order to give her daughter a strong connection to her and a feeling of love and security. This was a woman who put the welfare of her baby first—before herself, her relationship with her parents, her career, or material comfort. It was a sacrifice, but it paid off in a wonderful daughter who trusts people and is not afraid of intimacy.

Many pregnant women, however, lose faith in their own inner knowledge. They "blew it" by getting pregnant. They can no longer trust their intuition or instincts, so they listen to "authorities." "Don't be selfish," they are told. "Give your baby to someone who can really care for him." Even if they question the idea of anyone else's being able to take care of their babies as well as they would, they begin to feel selfish for even entertaining the idea of doing so. They are vulnerable and confused, and unscrupulous people take advantage of that vulnerability, thereby condemning both mother and child to lives of yearning and torment.

What Constitutes Security?

It is thus that society's tendency to be judgmental gets in the way of making good decisions. There needs to be a different attitude toward what makes children feel secure. Consider this story: A woman on the television program "Unsolved Mysteries" had always been perplexed by her fascination with stories and movies about prison. Only while reading or viewing these stories did she feel warm and secure. It was after finding her birthmother that she learned that she had spent the first ten months of her life in prison with her mother. She was not in a beautiful room, in an expensive home, in an exclusive neighborhood. She was in a small, perhaps dim room; but she was in the company of her mother, a mother who had plenty of time to love and bond with her before having to give her up for adoption. That ten-month period was the *only* time in her life that she felt secure! What does this tell us? What lesson can we learn from hearing this woman's story?

The Future of Adoption

What about adoption, then? If the separation trauma is so devastating for the child, what should we do? This is not an easy question to answer. It depends on many factors. Adoption is still the best solution for those children who would otherwise languish in foster care or orphanages. But the procurement of babies by some of the methods going on today is, in essence, the buying and selling of human lives. This is unconscionable.

Too often adoption facilitators are more concerned with socio-economic, rather than psychological, emotional, or intellectual considerations. There is a great deal more to preparing for an adopted child than fixing up a nursery or having enough money in the bank for a college education. There is a real need for emotional stability, honesty, and the willingness to become truly informed about what this process means for the adopting parents and for their child. Prospective adoptive parents must first make sure that the child they are about to adopt really *needs* to be adopted, and then they must ask themselves if they are really prepared emotionally and psychologically to meet the needs of that child.

Taking one of the truly needy children into one's home is a risky undertaking, because they have had so many separation traumas and may have been otherwise abused, emotionally, physically, or sexually. Rearing one of these children is a challenge which takes a mature, stable couple to meet. One has to be willing to sacrifice a great deal and expect nothing in return. (This does not mean that they will *get* nothing, just that they should expect nothing.) It is necessary for such a couple to know their own Achilles' heels, their own vulnerabilities, because these children will push all their buttons. This is a dilemma. Not everyone is cut out to adopt these children, yet they are the ones who truly need stable homes. A child needs the best chance at life that he can have, and no one has the ultimate answer as to what that might be. Someone once said, however, that before we do *anything* we should ask ourselves this question: "Is this good for our children?"

Lowering Expectations

We know that love is good for children, but in the case of adopted children, parents need to be realistic in their expectations of the adoptee's ability to accept love freely or to return it. Trust builds very slowly after a profound separation such as that which all adoptees experience. This is not a rejection of the person who is trying to give love; it is a way in which the child protects himself against further loss. This behavior makes a great deal of sense, yet at the same time it is difficult to accept.

Adoptive parents need to be assured that adopting a child is very important, and that they need not consider themselves failures as parents if their children seem unable to respond as they or others expect. The life of the family has begun with a handicap—their child's short, but profound, immediate postnatal history—a span of time which has largely been ignored by parents and professionals as having anything to do with what is going on in adoptive family life. Yet, in my opinion, *it is quintessential to understanding the dynamics of the adoptive family.*

Society's Attitudes Must Change

My purpose in writing this book is not to discourage adoption, but to add to the understanding of it. What each individual mother decides to do when she finds herself pregnant, she needs to do with the most information she can obtain about the whole concept of life and the mother/child relationship, as well as her own personal feelings, beliefs, and circumstances. And whatever her decision happens to be, she needs love and support from those closest to her.

Adoptees have a right to understand their own feelings, to have them validated, and to have the clinicians to whom they go for help understand their issues of abandonment and loss. Too many of them have been made to feel abnormal or crazy, when they have simply been responding to that early experience.

Every potential adoptive couple needs to be informed about the *primal wound* and the impact it will have on them, their child, and their child's biological mother. In preparing for their new child, they should explore their own issues of abandonment and loss. This includes the loss of their fertility, as well as losses resulting from death or divorce. All of these losses, if unresolved, may make them vulnerable and defensive about their child's feelings of rejection and loss. The best gift an adoptive couple can give their child is to work through their own issues of abandonment and loss (whatever form those issues took). The degree to which this has been accomplished will greatly affect how they act and react in their relationship to their child.

I realize that many people would be more comfortable if I were to end this book by painting a rosy picture of adoption and giving it a positive send-off, so to speak. But I can't, in good conscience, do that. Although adoption may be the best solution to the problem of children who cannot be kept by their biological parents, it is not like a fairy tale in which everyone lives "happily ever after." It is a difficult and complex process for everyone concerned. It deserves to be understood and honored as such. Denial and secrecy have no place in this process.

Talking about his adoption and his other family should be a part of every adoptee's relationship with his adoptive parents. This will in no way make them any less important to him. It will, instead, show him that they understand his feelings and his need to know about this heritage. Honesty and understanding will only serve to make the adoptive relationship stronger. One can force dependency upon another person, but one cannot force love and respect.

It is my hope that this book has contributed to the understanding of adoption as a life-long and complex process, which results in myriad issues to work through. The manner in which we respond to those issues will have a great deal to do with the developmental and emotional health of the adoptee, the emotional healing of his birth-mother, and the success of the adoptive family unit. Many of the suggestions herein can also be helpful in any family situation. The most important lesson may be that of validating a child's feelings and teaching him ways in which to respond responsibly to those feelings.

The Mystic Aspect

I will close with two unusual experiences, which were related to me by adoptees in the course of the early interviews. Both had to do with names and the timing of events, or what C. G. Jung calls synchronicity. These were the first of many such phenomena told to me over the years. They made me begin to wonder about the unconscious connection which might exist between an adoptee and his or her biological family. Both of these events happened to adoptees who had found their birth families.

In the first case, the adoptee's adoptive family decided to adopt another child when the adoptee was thirteen years old. As a way of making her feel a part of the new adoption process, the adoptive mother told her that she could name the baby. The baby was a girl, and she named her Diane. Years later, when she had found her birthmother, she discovered that exactly four years to the day of her own birthday, her birthmother had given birth to another little girl and had named her Diane. The adoptee had two sisters named Diane.

221

In the second story, the adoptee had finally found her birth father, after having been reunited with her mother for some time. (The adoptee had lived with both of them for the first four years of her life, until their divorce.) It was then that she discovered that her father had remarried and had a son, the adoptee's half brother. His name was Darrell, and he had died on the same day that her own daughter had been born. She had had no idea what to name her new baby and had just gone through a book of names until she came to Carol, but decided that that wasn't quite right. She kept going . . . Darrell. Yes, she would name her little girl Darrell. So, unknowingly, the new mother, giving birth on the day that her own brother died (a brother whose existence she had been unaware of), named her new daughter after him.

I found these two stories, and those which people have related to me since, fascinating. I wanted to end this book with them, because I am intrigued by the question: In just how many ways are we connected with those who came before us? And equally important: Why should anyone have the right to keep us from renewing those connections?

If we are going to put children first, we are going to have to face with courage and determination the truths about how our decisions impact these children. We are going to have to challenge our previously held ideas and deal with reality. No matter how difficult and painful it may be, acknowledging our vulnerabilities, limitations, and obstinacy in dealing with adoption is crucial to having more honest relationships with our children. Our children deserve it. We deserve it. Let us begin!

I've always wished that Moses had remained on Mt. Sinai a little longer and that God had given him an eleventh commandment: *Honor thy children.* Oh, what a different world it might be. . . .

GLOSSARY

attention deficit disorder (ADD) (n.) A syndrome with symptoms consisting of inattention, impulsivity, excessive motor activity, and an inability to set or achieve goals. If the disorder is present without hyperactivity, it may seem like day-dreaming.

avoidance (n.) A defense mechanism used in phobias and anxiety disorders in which one refuses to encounter or acknowledge situations or activities which represent some type of impulse, such as aggressive, angry, or sexual impulses, or the punishment for those impulses.

counterphobic (adj.) A condition whereby a person seeks the very situation of which they are afraid. An adoptee may run away, for instance, when his fear is that he will be abandoned.

denial (n.) A primitive defense mechanism in which one refuses to allow into consciousness a painful truth or unpleasant reality, such as a birthmother's being in denial about the pain of separation from her child. Denial is also used to refer to a more conscious form of resistance to reality, such as adoptive parents denying that adoptive families are different from biological families.

imago (n.) An image formed in the unconscious of someone which represents someone else, such as the mother imago. This imago may be an idealized image of the original person and may also be seen as an archetype.

intellectualize (v.) A means by which one can stave off feelings about a situation or experience by rational means, which makes one feel as if one has more control over experiences and their effects than is actually true. Intellectualization is used as a defense mechanism, most often to avoid painful feelings.

mirror (v.) To reflect back, especially with babies, children's own image of themselves so that they find that image to be positive. Mirroring, something that mothers do naturally, builds self-esteem in children.

narcissism (n.) Self-love, concern for self. Primary narcissism is a stage of human development when children are concerned with getting their needs met, have no concern for others, and harbor feelings of omnipotence. If a child does not get his needs met in childhood, narcissism may continue into adulthood and be considered pathological.

post-traumatic stress disorder (n.) A psychological diagnosis in which an atrocity is simultaneously or alternately relived in present circumstances or kept from consciousness by numbness of affect. This disorder is characterized by recurrent or intrusive recollections of the trauma, recurrent dreams of the event, feeling and acting as if the event were happening in the present because of "triggers" in the environment, withdrawing from the external world, hyperalertness, sleep disturbance, difficulty concentrating, or an intensifying of feelings during experiences which symbolize the traumatic event.

presenting problem (n.) The reason a potential patient gives for beginning psychotherapy. Although one's life may have been difficult for some time, it often takes a crisis or intolerable situation for a person to seek help. The presenting problem is usually only a symptom of some long-term, buried trauma or experience which is being reactivated in the present circumstances.

preverbal (adj.) Before having words for something. Preverbal feelings, such as those experienced by adoptees, are not easy to describe because they originated before the person could speak.

project (v.) To cast upon another person the attitudes, ideas, feelings, or impulses that belong to oneself. These attitudes or impulses are usually considered by the one projecting them to be undesirable or dangerous. This mechanism is often unconscious and is sometimes used as a means of handling internal conflict as if it were an external problem.

projective identification (n.) A means by which one makes one's feelings or pain known by acting in such a way as to cause another person to actually *feel* what the projector is feeling. Projective identification can be used as a defense mechanism, a form of communication, or a form of object relations. Acting-out children use projective identification to communicate to their parents the chaos, rage, and helplessness they feel inside.

repression (n.) A defense mechanism used to banish or eject painful memories, feelings, or impulses. Primal repression is that which has never been allowed up into consciousness. The early experience of separation from the mother and sexual molestation during infancy or early childhood are two examples of painful experiences which are often repressed.

Self (n.) The essence or core-being of a person giving one a sense of wholeness. The Self often gets lost as a result of early trauma and a feeling of having to act in such a way as to avoid re-experiencing that trauma. A person knows when he is acting from the true Self because there is a lack of anxiety and a feeling of congruency between the internal and external self.

suicidal ideation (n.) An idea to cause one's own death by suicide. Suicidal ideation may be accompanied by a plan for one's death, or it may be an obsession with the idea of death which is held in abeyance, like a door always kept open, as a *possible* means of avoiding painful feelings or situations. The "open door" interferes with healing by negating the need to confront painful feelings.

REFERENCES

Bettelheim, B. (1987). The Importance of Play. *Atlantic Monthly*, March 1987.

Bowlby, J. (1980). *Attachment and Loss* (Vol. III: Loss) New York: Basic Books.

Brazelton, T. B. (1982). Pre-birth memories appear to have lasting effect. *Brain/Mind Bulletin*, 7(5), 2.

Chamberlain, D. (1988). *Babies Remember Birth*. New York: Ballantine Books.

Clothier, F. (1943). The Psychology of the Adopted Child. *Mental Hygiene*, 27, 222-230.

Crichton, M. (1990). *Jurassic Park*. New York: Ballantine Books.

Donovan, D. & McIntyre, D. (1990). *Healing the Hurt Child*. New York: W. W. Norton & Company.

Erikson, E. (1950). *Childhood and Society*. New York: W. W. Norton & Company.

Frantz, G. (1985). Birth's cruel secret/O I my own lost mother/to my own sad child. *Chiron*, 157-171.

Greenacre, P. (1953). *Trauma, Growth and Personality*. London: Hogarth.

Grossenbacher, F. (1984). Personal interview.

Kaplan, S., Silverstein, D., Benward, J., & Melfeld, J. (1985). *Adoption: The Clinical Issues* (Workshop sponsored by Parenting Resources, Tustin, CA. and Post Adoption Center for Education and Research, Berkeley, CA.

Jung, C. G. *Collected Works*.

Kirk, D. (1964). *Shared Fate*. New York: Free Press.

Liedloff, J. (1975). *The Continuum Concept*. New York: Warner Books.

Lifton, B. J. (1975). *Twice Born*. New York: McGraw-Hill.

Machtiger, J. (1985). Perilous beginnings: Loss, abandonment, and transformation. *Chiron*, 101-129.

Maduro, R. (1985). Abandonment and deintegration of the primary self. *Chiron*, 131-156.

Mahler, M., Pine, F., & Bergman, A. (1975). *The Psychological Birth of the Human Infant*. New York: Basic Books.

Neumann, E. (1973). *The Child*. New York: G. P. Putnam.

Nickman, S. (1985). Losses in adoption: The need for dialogue. *Psychoanalytic Study of the Child*, *37*, 365-398.

Pearce, J. C. (1977) *Magical Child*. New York: Bantam Books.

Richo, D. (1992). *How to Be an Adult*. New Jersey: Paulist Press.

Scarf, M. (1987). *Intimate Partners*. New York: Random House.

Sorosky, A., Baran, A. & Pannor, R. (1978). *The Adoption Triangle*. New York: Anchor Press.

Stern, D. (1985). *The Interpersonal World of the Infant*. New York: Basic Books.

Stone, F. (1972). Adoption and identity. *Child Psychiatry and Human Development*, *2*(3), 120-128.

Taichert, L., & Harvin, D. (1975). Adoption and children with learning problems. *The Western Journal of Medicine*, *122*(6), 464-470.

Viorst, J. (1986). *Necessary Losses*. New York: Ballantine Books.

Wickes, F. (1927, 1955, 1966, 1991). *The Inner World of Childhood*. New York: Spectrum Books.

Wieder, H. (1978). Special problems in the psychoanalysis of adopted children. In J. Glenn (Ed.), *Child Analysis and Therapy*, 557-577.

Winnicott, D. (1966). *The Family and Individual Development*. New York: Basic Books.

_____ (1974). Fear of breakdown. *International Review of Psycho-Analysis*, *1*, 103-107.

SUGGESTED READING

Benzola, E. *Temporary Child: A Foster Care Survivor's Story*

Blau, E. *Stories of Adoption: Loss and Reunion*

Brodzinsky, Schecter, & Henig. *Being Adopted*

Carlini, H. *Birth Mother Trauma*

Demuth, C. *Courageous Blessing - Adoptive Parents and the Search*

Estes, C. *Women Who Run with the Wolves*

Gediman, J. & Brown, L. *BirthBond*

Gunderson, T. *How to Locate Anyone Anywhere*

Hendrix, H. *Getting the Love You Want*

Herman, J. *Trauma and Recovery*

Jones, M.B. *Birthmothers: Women Who Have Relinquished Babies for Adoption Tell Their Stories*

Lerner, H. *The Dance of Anger*

_____ *The Dance of Intimacy*

Liedloff, J. *The Continuum Concept*

Lifton, B.J. *Journey of the Adopted Self*

_____ *Lost and Found*

McColm, M. *Adoption Reunions*

Melina, L. *Raising Adopted Children*

Melina, L. & Roszia, S. *The Open Adoption Experience*

Miller, A. *Drama of the Gifted Child*

Moore, T. *Care of the Soul*

Moses, S. *Dear Mom, I've found my birthmother*

Pearce, J. C. *Evolution's End*

Riben, M. *The Dark Side of Adoption*

Richo. D. *How to Be an Adult*

Schaefer. C. *The Other Mother*

Seligman. M. *Learned Optimism*

Severson. R.W. *Adoption: Charms and Rituals for Healing*

Sexson. L. *Ordinarily Sacred*

Solinger. R. *Wake Up Little Susie*

Sorosky. Baran. & Pannor. *The Adoption Triangle*

Stiffler. L. *Synchronicity and Reunion*

Tavris. C. *Anger*

Verny. T. *Secret Life of the Unborn Child*

Viorst. J. *Necessary Losses*

Welch. M. *Holding Time*

Zweig. C. & Abrams. J. (Eds.) *Meeting the Shadow*

ABOUT THE AUTHOR

Nancy Verrier, M.A., the mother of two daughters—one who is adopted and one who is not—is an advocate for children. She holds a master's degree in clinical psychology and is in private practice in Lafayette, California. In addition to her clinical and adoption work, Ms. Verrier writes and lectures about the effects of early childhood trauma and deprivation caused by premature separation from the mother under various circumstances.